Just Playing'?

THE ROLE AND STATUS OF PLAY IN
EARLY CHILDHOOD EDUCATION

Janet R. Moyles

OPEN UNIVERSITY PRESS
Milton Keynes • Philadelphia

Open University Press
Celtic Court
22 Ballmoor
Buckingham MK18 1XW

and
1900 Frost Road, Suite 101
Bristol, PA 19007, USA

First Published 1989
Reprinted 1990, 1991 (twice)

British Library Cataloguing in Publication Data

Moyles, Janet R.
  Just playing?: the role and status of play in
  early childhood education
  1. Learning by children. Role of play
  I. Title
  155.4′13
  ISBN 0-335-09569-0
  ISBN 0-335-09564-X (pbk)

Library of Congress Cataloging-in-Publication Data

Moyles, Janet R.
  Just playing?: the role and status of play in early childhood
education/Janet R. Moyles.
      p.   cm.
  Bibliography: p.
  Includes index.
  ISBN 0-335-09569-0   ISBN 0-335-09564-X (pbk.)
  1. Play.   2. Early childhood education.   I. Title
LB1140.35.P55M69 1989
371-21--dc20   89-3327   CIP

Typeset by Burns and Smith, Derby
Printed in Great Britain by The Alden Press, Oxford

Just Playing?

To Brian, Neil and Ian, the players and playmates in my own scenario.

Contents

Acknowledgements

The ideas, notions, thoughts and experiences one has over the years in education and teaching are come by as a result of many interactions with many different people, some of them committed to memory for ever, some absorbed and assimilated as part of your very own being. So it is with thoughts and actions regarding play. The contributions made by so many people – children and adults alike – in both playing and talking about play have had a profound influence, and I sincerely acknowledge their contribution.

What really forces one into defining one's own perspectives is in trying to teach other people about the subject. In this case it was children's play in school, and I would like to thank the growing number of postgraduate certificate of education (PGCE) students whom I have had the pleasure of teaching and who have taught me so much and contributed in so many ways to my own understanding. In particular, I thank Sue Lambarth, who instigated the idea for Fig. 7.5 and all of her year-group for their contributions to my own thinking on play. In addition, the contribution of Kathy Bond is acknowledged in inspiring some of the ideas for problem solving in Chapter 4.

I should also like to thank the children, parents and staff and heads of the various schools who welcomed me and gave me access in order to take photographs and notes of different incidents and to Jane Hislam who made valuable contributions to my photographic collection as well as being a very supportive colleague. I should also like to acknowledge my gratitude for the listening skills and advice of Margaret Naylor and the general support of Brian Moyles.

Introduction

Play is undoubtedly a means by which humans and animals explore a variety of experiences in different situations for diverse purposes. Consider, for example, when one acquires a new item of equipment, such as a washing machine – a majority of adults will dispense with the formality of reading the manual from cover to cover in favour of 'playing' with the controls and functions. By this means, individuals come to terms with innovations and familiarize themselves with objects and materials: in descriptions of child play this is frequently classed as 'functional' play. This 'hands on' experience of a real situation with a real purpose for the would-be 'player' is normally followed by the immediate learning of many of the facets of the new machine, reinforced subsequently by referral to the manual and consolidated by practice.

The similarity of this process to an idealized form of learning for young children is inescapable. Yet how far is play truly valued by those involved with the education and upbringing of young children? How often is play and choosing play materials reserved as an activity for when children have finished their 'work', thus reducing both its impact and its effect on the child's development? How many children come to nursery education unable to involve themselves in play because of a passive upbringing which has viewed play as a noisy, messy and unnecessary activity?

What most adults fail to recognize and acknowledge is just how much they themselves play in adult life, and unless and until we can both accept such play *and* value it in its many forms, it is difficult for anyone to value children's play as anything other than a non-work activity.

Take as another example, role play. Children explore what it is like to be mother, father, doctor, dentist (Plowden Report: DES, 1967: para. 523): wearing another's shoes helps children to deal with polymorphous characters in a range of contexts and is typified in pretend and dramatic play. Many adults find it difficult to consider themselves as instigators of such role play except perhaps as active participants in a professional or amateur dramatic production. But what of the prospective applicant for a

Plate 1. Wearing another's 'shoes' helps children to deal with polymorphous characters in a range of contexts, and is typified in pretend and dramatic play.

new job? Most of us ascertain, before an interview, through reading the job descriptions and talking to people with knowledge of the institution or organization, just what kind of person is being sought. Prior to and during the interview, at least in the early stages, we attempt to play the role we believe conforms to the expectations of the interviewers. This is not denying oneself as a unique individual but simply part and parcel of the make-up of being an adaptable and worthy adult.

Children and adults all wear different 'hats' in different situations and it is perfectly acceptable that they do. By doing so, each grows to an understanding of the real 'self' and self-worth (Holt, 1972). Parents and teachers prime children to use appropriate behaviour for different purposes and audiences. Adults consciously and unconsciously modify their presentation of themselves dependent upon whether the recipient of their attention is a member of the family, the vicar or the boss! Play, therefore, has a context, an appropriateness and a register which should offer it status as with any other essentially human trait. Stone (1982:10) views play as a very high priority: 'Play is recreation ... because it continually re-creates the society in which it is carried on.'

Play at its best in educational situations, provides not only a real medium for learning but enables discerning and knowledgeable adults to learn about children and their needs. In the school context, this means teachers being able to understand where children 'are' in their learning and general development which, in turn, gives educators the starting point for promoting new learning in both cognitive and affective domains.

In this book, the concern is not to create yet another definition of play: adults know what they consider play to be and there are enough books on the subject such as those by Hutt (1966), Millar (1968), Garvey (1977), Smith (1984) and Cohen (1987) to which reference can be made. Rather, an attempt will be made to challenge conceptions of what play in the school context can and should provide for young learners. This is vital in an educational climate where a subject-based, core curriculum and its content could well relegate the vital issue of play in educational contexts to the bottom of any ladder of importance. Adults will require strength, knowledge and a carefully conceived argument on play philosophy and practice in order to maintain its vital position in early childhood education. The emphasis throughout is on 4- to 8-year-olds, whose play is such a vital part of development, and social and intellectual learning. The words of El'Kounin (1982) seem to sum up this aspect beautifully within this age range. He emphasizes:

> In play the child operates with things as things having meaning; he operates with the meanings of words which substitute for the thing; therefore, in play, there occurs the emancipation of the word from the thing. (El'Kounin, 1982:230)

Essentially, the book is in three parts. Part One deals with an overview of play as a construct and outlines some theoretical considerations in relation to play as a learning medium, establishing models for both play (Chapter 1) and learning (Chapter 2). Part One, then, explores some of the many reasons why play occurs, itemizes a few different ways of considering and categorizing play in a variety of contexts and generally sets the scene for succeeding chapters.

With core curriculum matters a priority, the processes of education are sometimes overlooked and subject-based learning becomes paramount. Rather than take a curriculum-based view *per se*, I have chosen, in Part Two, to look at the three areas of language, problem solving and creativity, embracing as they do both the processes and products of education and especially play.

A rather more pragmatic stance is taken in Part Three, which deals with various approaches to making provision for play in the early years, relates it to basic curriculum and classroom organization (Chapter 6), observing learning, progression and assessment (Chapter 7), children's individual needs (Chapter 8) and the role of parents and other adults (Chapter 9). The final chapter reviews the whole question of children's and adults' play, summarizes the main contents and raises a few further considerations.

The pattern adopted for most chapters will be to take examples of play situations in the early years curriculum and explore the apparent or potential learning within each situation. The discussion will then be broadened to investigate developmental and theoretical issues inherent in the particular play activities and incorporate suggestions for initiating and sustaining children's participation and learning in associated play activities. Throughout, practical observations and suggestions will be supported and enhanced by reference to relevant literature and previous research, thus allowing readers the opportunity to pursue aspects of particular interest.

Many adults pay lip-service to play. This book, although focusing mainly on early childhood educators, aims to help students, teachers, nursery nurses, parents and all those who influence the lives of children to see how play can be truly utilized for development and learning throughout life. For, as Loizos (1969:275) strongly asserts:

Far from being a 'spare-time', superfluous activity ... it may be that play at certain crucial early stages is necessary for the occurrence and success of all later social activity.

PART ONE

1
Unravelling the 'Mystery' of Play

Scenarios

1. A 4-year-old child, dressed in a home-made garment of silky material and net, draped around her and reminiscent of a cross between a normal dance dress and a tutu, pirouetting in front of the dressing-up mirror, standing on one foot, attempting 'points' while holding out the net skirt in one hand and humming a nursery rhyme to herself.

2. An adult on the telephone, pad and pen to hand, draws a curved line and adds to it systematically until, after 5 minutes, the page is beautifully decorated with scrolls and circles – some imitative of faces, some simply abstract forms.

3. A dog playing with a rubber bone, tossing it into the air or at any attentive audience with no obvious intention of doing anything specific with it, chasing and pouncing upon it when thrown, returning it doggedly, nosing it, rolling over beside it, daring anyone to remove it yet baiting them to do so!

As you consider these play behaviours, the most vital question which is likely to spring to mind is, inevitably:

Why do humans and animals play?

Over a century of research has produced many speculative thoughts as to why play occurs but little conclusive agreement as to what play really is (Gardner and Gardner, 1975). From the examples above, it is clear that play is at least a recognizable phenomena and has a significance to the participants, but does it confer any advantages on those who undertake it? Would we be, in some measure, less of a person or animal without it? Perhaps two even more necessary questions would be:

Why do humans (and many higher animals) find it so difficult NOT to play?

What does play provide which is apparently so intrinsically satisfying?

Teachers and others involved in the education and care of young children must approach these questions, effectively and thoroughly analysing their own thoughts regarding play and the role and status they assign to it. More importantly, they must investigate and establish to their own satisfaction, what is meant by play. Only by doing this will adults be able to make the kind of provision they deem acceptable: it is a recognized 'fact' in education that successful teaching and learning of anything is highly dependent on the teacher being convinced of the merits of a particular philosophy, method or style.

The problem seems to be that play research has become swamped in a morass of definitions of play as a basis for supporting later arguments. Laudable though it is to try to define play, this does perhaps suggest a quantifiable approach which, in practice, has rarely been the case. As Smith (1984:68) points out: 'a definition of play is important.... This does not mean that a single or all-embracing definition is easy, or attainable, or even desirable.' While accepting almost instinctively the value of play, it has been difficult for teachers involved in the day-to-day organization of children's learning, to extract anything of sufficient pragmatic and theoretical substance on which to base their judgements and learning provision. Justification for play activities in an educational context is really much harder to establish than research such as the practical study by Manning and Sharp (1977) or the useful background theoretical studies of Bruner *et al.* (1977) implicitly suggest.

Ample evidence of this difficulty exists in infant and first schools where 'play' is often relegated to activities, toys and games children can choose when they have finished their 'work'. How often do teachers establish it as part of their teaching role, and they themselves become engaged in the chosen play – despite much research such as that by Sylva *et al.* (1980), advocating the need for teacher interaction and intervention at opportune moments to ensure optimum value in play?

The dichotomy for teachers is very real: on the one hand, the implication is that children learn very little without teacher direction, yet, on the other hand, children's self-initiated play is advocated (Tamburrini, 1982) as providing the best learning context. This simply serves to highlight the many complexities of the early childhood educator's role. Time spent in playing with children is less time spent on, say, hearing individual's read, and vice versa! There is also the difficulty, highlighted by Sutton-Smith (1986) and Strom (1981a), that adults themselves actually find it very unsatisfying and even frustrating to play with children (a point which will be taken up further in Chapter 9).

What appears to be required is the opportunity for teachers to develop a sound construct of play which has an academic rigour acceptable to all those involved as a justification for its practical existence in primary schools. It must satisfy parents and others, who may feel that children can participate in all the play they need in other contexts external to school, e.g. at home or in the local park. Inherent in the following chapters is the opportunity for teachers and others to explore their thinking based on certain premises, some of which have already been outlined and many of which have yet to reveal themselves. In no sense am I attempting to reformulate a theory of play behaviours and stances. Rather, the attempt is to put some of the existing knowledge into a context and framework with which early educators can empathize and use as a basis for their own reflections and considerations of play.

There is, therefore, now a need to return to the earlier questions and examine some of the issues in greater depth.

Why play?

Taking in turn the three examples which began this chapter, we can start to examine the wider implications of the play represented in these cameos from everyday life.

The young child taking on the role of a dancer is experimenting with what it is like to adopt the role of someone else. She imitates movements, mannerisms, gestures, expressions: she actually feels what it is like to be dressed in stiff net-like material, the contrasting textures, the properties it provides and the different qualities and physical stances it inspires. Through the mirror, she examines herself in another guise, probably stimulated further by various factors such as the bright cerise colour of the underlying material and the creamy white contrast of the net, the different shape given to her outline form by this special garment and how she 'fits' into the picture presented by the mirror image. In pirouetting, she is exploring her own physical abilities, tentatively and clumsily at first but with rapidly increasing poise and agility. She is not attempting to *be* that dancer and is still firmly grounded in the world of childhood, evidenced by humming a nursery rhyme. Of this type of play, Garvey (1977:88) asserts:

> Some enactments [of roles] are schematic, representing only salient events in a sequence of actions.... Most enactments are clearly created from concepts of appropriate behaviour and are most likely not direct imitations of people.

The adult doodling, is exploring the medium available in ways either previously undiscovered or as a conscious or unconscious repetition of a design previously encountered, or variations on a theme. This may have a purpose or not, dependent on the particular adult and the individual role with which they are normally associated, such as that of a graphic artist, hobbyist painter or calligrapher. A main feature is that this type of exploratory play which, according to Hutt (1966), is a preliminary to actual play, will only be a preliminary to play if the person engages in calligraphy or painting as a hobby. If this is a job, and therefore has an end-product, by most people's thinking it would then cease to be play. This highlights particularly the difficulties when play and work are viewed as polar extremes, a worthy consideration for later in this chapter.

The dog is practising his own skills and abilities some of which may, in an undomesticated environment, have helped him to gain mastery over a moving object intended as food. His associated wide-gaped grin is, according to Attenborough (1988), a typical feature of mammalian play and signals to others the non-threat context of the play 'attack'. His persistence is rewarded in terms of his own growing skills and in encouraging another to play with him, thus creating a social rough-and-tumble play situation. A tug-of-war exercise with the rubber bone enables him to estimate his own strength and agility, try out playful aggression on another and gauge responses to his actions. Immediately he nips a hand in error he wants to make amends by licking it and wagging his tail to show that all is well and that it was unintentional.*

These simple examples of play represent many different levels of complexity and provide a range of potential learning situations. Surprisingly, perhaps, the child's play is by far the most complex, involving the child as it does in abstraction and decentred thinking (Donaldson, 1978). Many studies have concluded that this type of imitative play in animal and human species is the most highly advanced form along play–complex continuum (e.g. Lancy, 1981) and in humans reflects higher-order thinking and organization. Millar (1968:156) suggests that role play:

> belongs with all those processes and structures which underlie the coding, storing, checking and recoding of information and which appear to keep the human brain pretty constantly busy.

Isaacs (1930), on the other hand, firmly believes that, through role play in particular, the child is able to resolve inner conflict and anxiety.

---

* This chapter contains the sole reference to play in animals. It has served the purpose of facilitating exploration of a particular type of play and allowed comparisons to be drawn between animals and humans. Although there is much to be learnt from the play of animals, limitations of space and the focus of this book on young children's play in the context of school, renders any further examination of animal behaviours inappropriate. Readers interested in investigating animal play further should consult any of the following texts: Groos (1898), Morris (1969) Bruner *et al.* (1977) and Smith (1984).

The adult's play appears to be in response to an internal demand to occupy oneself mentally and physically while another well-mastered activity is taking place. Like the child's play, in this instance, it is solitary. The dog's play satisfies his need for interaction with others in a physical and enjoyable social setting.

Perhaps, therefore, one answer to the question 'Why play?' is that it ensures the brain – and in children nearly always the body – is stimulated and active. This, in turn, motivates and challenges the participant both to master what is familiar and to respond to the unfamiliar in terms of gaining information, knowledge, skills and understandings. In the play of older children and adults, this is clearly manifested in games activities of diverse kinds such as chess and sports. In younger children, play is positively associated with general development and maturation (Millar, 1968). At all ages, play is undertaken for sheer pleasure and enjoyment and engenders a cheerful attitude to life and learning. This latter is surely sufficient reason on its own for play to be valued. As Tinbergen (1976:12) ruefully points out, in Western societies 'the mood everywhere around the children has become so serious'. Yet equally, as pointed out by Prosser (1985:174), necessary activities for children and adults can be enjoyed without them being play.

This emphasis on enjoyment is very much at the crux of the next question: 'What advantages does play confer?', which in turn, is linked inextricably with 'What does play provide?'

Few would deny that play, in all its forms, has the advantage of providing fun and enjoyment. Piers and Landau (1980:43) go so far as to say play 'develops creativity, intellectual competence, emotional strength and stability and ... feelings of joy and pleasure: the habit of being happy'. Conversely, it seems that play can and does occur in the context of resolving conflict and anxiety (see Isaacs, 1930) which is seemingly contradictory. However, consider this statement by Garvey (1977:32):

A new experience, if not frightening, is likely first to attract attention, then exploration. Only after a novel feature of the environment has been investigated can it be treated more lightly and enjoyed.

This serves yet again to emphasize the complexity of the construct of play or, put another way, when is play not play! Hutt (1979) firmly distinguishes exploration from play and presents many valuable and persuasive arguments to support this view. Perhaps it is most useful to define exploration (such as that which one undertakes with a new piece of equipment or encounter) as a vital prerequisite to a deeper, more challenging play experience when all the variables of an object or situation begin to be understood. Most people would agree that they begin to enjoy experiences to a greater extent when a certain level of familiarity is achieved. Sometimes even, after what was not at the time an enjoyable experience, there is joy in relating its detail and outcome to others. Enjoyment, therefore, although important and motivating in itself, needs some qualification, and in Chapter 2 I will return to this point more fully in examining play and learning.

Stimulation, variety, interest, concentration and motivation are equally provided by the play situation (as well as others). If one adds to this the opportunity to be part of an experience which, although quite possibly demanding, is unthreatening and free from irrelevant constraint and which allows the participant a meaningful interaction within his or her own environment, the advantages of play become even more apparent. Play can, however, also provide an escape, sometimes from the pressures of reality, occasionally to relieve boredom and sometimes simply as relaxation or opportunity for solitude often denied adults and children in the busy day-to-day environment. For although the social qualities of play are nearly always those which gain paramountcy in thinking about the concept, it is and should be accepted as something private and internal to the individual when that is their choice. This applies equally to children in the whirl of activities in school and at home and a point which will be returned to in Chapter 8 when individual needs are considered in relation to play.

The list of advantages arising from play is growing rapidly but has still to incorporate so many factors. Play helps the participants to build confidence in themselves and their abilities and, in social situations, helps them to judge the many variables within social interactions and gain empathy with others. It leads to children and adults developing perceptions about other people and understanding the two-way demands of expectation and tolerance. Opportunities to explore such concepts as freedom implicitly exist in many play situations and lead eventually to providing bridging points in the development of independence. At a more basic level, play provides situations in which skills can be practised, both physical and mental, and repeated as many times as is necessary for confidence and mastery. In addition, it affords an opportunity to explore one's own potentialities and limitations. Stallibrass (1974) sees the development of flexibility and spontaneity as a most vital function of play. Froebel, as long ago as 1826, saw the value of play as lying in the opportunities it provides for sensory experiences which, in turn he believed, are the foundation of intellectual development. Upon just such a premise, early educators have valued play for well over a century.

The question posed earlier as to whether we might be somehow less of a child or adult and suffer some kind of deprivation without play, must surely be yes, for in what other ways can we have the kinds of opportunities just outlined? The major problem is that to prove such a

Plate 2. Play provides activities in which skills can be practised, both physical and mental, and repeated as many times as is necessary for confidence and mastery.

theory requires children to be deprived of the opportunity – an unacceptable proposition. However, work with handicapped children, prevented from normal play by their disabilities, has emphasized the relative deprivation in terms of sensory experiences (see Newson *et al.*, 1973; Wall, 1961). It is true that non-play situations can provide some experiences but these tend to rely on greater formality and less facility for people to express themselves and their own qualities. This is particularly the case with children whose expression in other ways, for example, verbal language, is limited by their immaturity and stage of development. The reader is encouraged to reflect on any one full working day and ask themselves at what points in the day their concentration wandered from the task at hand and what they did to remotivate themselves?

Play and work

Undoubted differences lie in these two concepts but are they really so diverse? Let us look at one or two points from the list of play advantages above and contrast them with work-oriented features:

- Do you ever enjoy your work?
- Do you feel stimulated and excited by it?
- Does it provide you with variety and challenge?
- Do you experience interactions with others?
- Do you learn about dealing with other people?
- Does work tell you anything about your own skills and abilities?
- Does it give you an opportunity to repeat necessary actions or responses?

Conversely, do you ever work at your play, for example work at winning the badminton match, work for the satisfaction of completing a garment, write poetry for the sheer love of words or paint, not only as personal expression, but for the satisfaction of having your own works of art around you? If the answer to any of these two sets of questions is yes, then what makes your work different from many facets of your play? According to Hans (1981:26):

> People who believe in the work ethic do so because their work is also play for them and is also a central area in their lives where playful interaction with the world takes place.... People still play on the job no matter how alienated they are from their labour.

The main argument forwarded by play purists, is that play occurs for no real purpose and has no overt goal (see Garvey, 1977). However, other researchers, notably several of those who have written under the editorship of Tizard and Harvey (1977), argue that play in itself is and can be directed towards goals of the participant's will whether that person be adult or child. Hans (1981:xi) links play, production and desire, saying 'play always involves and is always a part of production and desire'. According to Millar (1968), what characterizes play is that it is within the person's own control and planning, though Mussen *et al.* (1965:269) states that this should not be in response to 'pressing environmental demands'.

Not only is there this dilemma as to play and purpose but the added difficulty of its parameters and quality. As stressed by Kalverboer (1977:121), there are vast individual differences in the types and quality of children's play which, if it is to be understood and analysed, needs to be capable of observation despite the inevitable complexity of doing so. It seems apparent that different forms of play represent different challenges and it is just this variety which renders play so difficult to define. Categories of play always manage to appear discreet in a way that the reality clearly shows they are not. Consider, for a moment, the identification of play categories as identified in Table 1.1. For the sake of clarity, the list cannot be exhaustive but, as a prerequisite to future thinking about play, it is essential. Bear in mind, however, the warning of

Burghardt (1984:5): 'it must be acknowledged at the outset that many questions of recognising, describing and classifying play are still unresolved'.

It is clear that one could argue about the merits of this list, what is included and excluded, for a long time to come. But accepting that play is a natural part of all our lives and has value both for children and adults, as previously explored, we now have a basis for our deliberations, at least in relation to education.

One main stance of this book is that play *must* be viewed as a process. This view is epitomized in the writing of Bruner (1977:v):

> For the main characteristic of play – whether of child or adult – is not its content but its mode. Play is an approach to action, not a form of activity.

If one accepts play as process, it is obvious that a satisfactory definition will be elusive. Try to define, for example, the process of falling in love: immediately one is struck by the many variables of the situation and the kind of personal chemistry involved. The quality of any child's play is likely to be equally dependent upon as many variables, not least of which will be the value the child and others attach to it. Talking to early years teachers, it seems almost instinctive for them to say that play is valuable. Writers have told us so for more than 100 years now, from Froebel onwards, and the changing concepts of childhood have confirmed this belief. Teachers frequently rue the fact that parents do not appear to value play activities in the curriculum, yet, as discussed previously, they themselves implicitly foster this notion in their organization of class activities.

Is it not feasible and quite acceptable, however, that parents are, in fact, correct to question the types of play situations frequently found in schools? As consumers, do they not have rights to expect play in school to be different from the type of play engaged in by their children at home and elsewhere? Is it not easier for parents to provide 'good' play outside school if they are *not* trying to compete with school play? (It is only necessary to refer readers to the reading scheme book syndrome for them to understand what is meant!) Should they not be able to see for themselves that play in school has greater rigour and is more academically oriented?

There is no doubt that such research as that by Manning and Sharp (1977) provides teachers with a good framework for considering provision for children's play, yet in selecting the word 'structuring' in relation to play there is the suggestion that any other kind of play than that provided by the teacher is 'unstructured'. The notion of structured/unstructured play has not altogether been a helpful one for early years teachers and has perhaps created classrooms where, because of the many difficulties and

Table 1.1. Different forms of play in school.

Basic form		Detail	Examples
PHYSICAL PLAY	Gross motor	Construction Destruction	Building blocks Clay/sand/wood
	Fine motor	Manipulation Coordination	Interlocking bricks Musical instruments
	Psychomotor	Adventurous Creative movement Sensory exploration Object play	Climbing apparatus Dance Junk modelling Finding out table
INTELLECTUAL PLAY	Linguistic	Communication/function/ explanation/acquisition	Hearing/telling stories
	Scientific	Exploration/investigation/ problem solving	Water play/cooking
	Symbolic/mathematical	Representation/pretend/ mini-worlds/	Doll's house/homes/ drama/number games
	Creative	Aesthetics/imagination fantasy/reality/ innovation	Painting/drawing/ modelling/ designing

SOCIAL/ EMOTIONAL PLAY		
Therapeutic	Aggression/regression/ relaxation/solitude/ parallel play	Wood/clay/music
Linguistic	Communication/interaction cooperation	Puppets/telephone
Repetitious	Mastery/control	Anything!
Empathic	Sympathy/sensitivity	Pets/other children
Self-concept	Roles/emulation/ morality/ethnicity	Home corner/service 'shop'/discussion
Gaming	Competition/rules	Word/number games

Note that there is significant overlap in all areas, impossible to represent in figurative form. Readers may like to construct a 'play wheel', three overlapping but decreasing sized circles, marked off in wedges, each wedge containing the basic and detailed headings shown above, which can be rotated within each other, which represent more adequately the relationship between areas.

dilemmas in providing structured play wherein the teacher participates or interacts as Manning and Sharp suggest, challenging play is not occurring in any real sense at all.

The impracticality of it with a class of 30 or more begins to defeat even the most dynamic of practitioners. But if, for a moment, we think about play in general in any classroom or, indeed, any situation where different forms of play occur, one thing becomes quite apparent: play is *always* structured by the materials that the participants have available to them. Sand is heaped up or made into pies dependent upon (a) having the sand there, either on the beach or in the sand tray, and (b) whether or not you have only your hands or some kind of container available to you. Wobbly towers can be constructed with stacking construction toys, whereas an interlocking brick system will allow for the greater stability and cohesion of a building.

If all play, then, is structured by the materials and resources available, the quality of any play will, in part, be dependent upon the quality and perhaps controlled quantity and variety of what is provided. This has enormous connotations for teachers and others involved in early education because it means considering at some length and in some depth exactly what, at any time, they require children to gain from a particular play situation, such as the home corner, and changing the provision of resources and materials regularly to account for this.

The question then becomes not so much one of structure but of whether the children will be allowed *free* play or be *directed*. As was emphasized earlier, access to free play – that is the opportunity to explore and investigate materials and situations for oneself – can be forerunner to more challenging play. It can and should, however, also be the sequel to it. An actual example that I witnessed might help to clarify this.

A new material, Polydron, was introduced to a group of 6-year-olds. The set consisted of plastic squares and triangles which interlocked along the edges in a rather novel way, something like a dovetail joint in woodwork. The children were given the opportunity for *free* play with the materials on a number of occasions, the time-scale being dependent upon how long it took the individual children to explore the material before they appeared to understand and were familiar with its properties, qualities and possible functions. The teacher herself then constructed a cube of Polydron squares, one of which comprised a hinged lid. She asked the children if they could make a similar 'box' and in so doing had, on this occasion, involved the children in *directed* play. The children readily constructed their own cubes discussing colour, shape, number of pieces, what made the lid hinge, and so on. Their efforts were discussed with and praised by the teacher, and the material was then tidied away for another occasion. When that other occasion arose the children were again allowed an opportunity for free play and they returned to making cubes with

Plate 3. The quality of any play will, in part, be dependent upon the quality and perhaps controlled quantity and variety of what is provided.

hinged lids, this time with small plastic play-people inside! This prompted one child to change her lid by adding another square to the top and propping one square against the other to make a roof: free play and new learning in one go!

The first session of free play allowed exploration, the second allowed a degree of mastery. With this came the opportunity for at least one child to add some new learning. The directed play by the teacher channelled the exploration and learning from the free play and took the children a stage further forward from where they then were in terms of understanding: surely the essence of good teaching? As can be seen, the suggestion is that the process is actually cyclical by extending into a spiral of play and learning modelled in Fig. 1.1. Rather like a pebble on a pond, the ripples from the exploratory free play through directed play and back to enhanced and enriched free play, allowed a spiral of learning spreading ever outwards into wider experiences for the children and upwards into the accretion of knowledge and skills. In defining play in this way, we are hopefully allowing ourselves to see its greater potential, freeing it from the constraints imposed by thinking too didactically about structure.

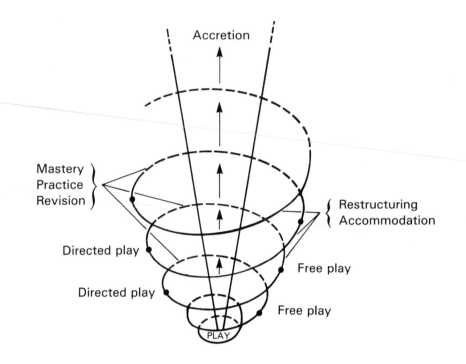

Fig. 1.1. The play spiral.

Perhaps all adults involved in the care and education of young children, would be able to think about play more clearly if we could rise above semantics! As Peacocke (1987:3) laments: 'It is unfortunate that the word "play" has so many definitions, parents are suspicious of it.' Many people would agree that there is an urgent need for a different terminology – play has all too often been used to infer something rather trivial and non-serious, the polar extreme to work rather than, as in a child context, the essence of serious, concentrated thinking (Brierley, 1987) and one purposeful means to learning. Thinking about free and directed play activity could possibly provide a solution.

At the heart of what is play in relation to schooling lies the notion of the appropriateness of the teacher's role. Should free play occur in schools? Perhaps not, if the view of 'teacher' is as an instructor or an imparter of knowledge. However, within a notion of teacher as enabler and initiator of learning, free and directed play are essential features of the teacher/child interaction, because the teacher both allows and provides necessary and appropriate resources. The materials and resources presented to children in school often differ significantly from those in the home, e.g. which homes have attribute blocks as standard equipment? (One could, incidentally, argue for some time on the merits of this, but it would not in fact take away the reality.) The different materials will give both a different status and different structure to the play situations. Rightly, because of these differences, children must be allowed the opportunity to experience, explore and investigate materials for themselves and, at least in the first few instances, make what they will of it. Only when that first-hand exploration has occurred, should adults consider using the material in a directed situation. As Sava (1975:13) suggests, if a child refuses the directed play he or she is unlikely to be ready for it.

Putting this different perspective on play and relating it instead to classroom activity might well help adults come to terms with some of the conflicts inherent in the whole construct of play.

Reiterating, then, the main principles of this chapter on which the rest of the book is based, are that:

1. Play must be accepted as a process, not necessarily with any outcome but capable of one if the participant so desires.
2. Play is necessary for children and adults.
3. Play is not the obverse of work; both are part of all of our lives.
4. Play is always structured by the environment, the materials or contexts in which it takes place.
5. Exploration is a preliminary to more challenging forms of play which, in the school environment, are those likely to be directed by the teacher.
6. Appropriately directed play will ensure the child learns from his or her current state of knowledge and skill.
7. Parents have a right to expect that play in school should be significantly and differently organized from play at home and elsewhere. If it can be shown to be so, they are more likely to attach value and importance to it.
8. Play is potentially an excellent learning medium.

Chapter 2 will now explore this last principle.

2

Play and Learning

Scenarios

1. Two 5-year-olds with small wooden constructional blocks are observed building the shapes upwards randomly until they fall down. This is repeated several times with growing excitement. Eventually, Child 1 begins jumping on the fallen structure, giggling loudly and holds the hand of Child 2 in encouragement to do the same. Persuaded, Child 2 jumps and giggles also but, in the process, pushes the other child over accidentally. Child 1 immediately responds by kicking Child 2 quite hard. Both cry and rub their injuries. Child 2 kicks out at a few unfallen bricks, which promptly tumble interestingly to the ground. Child 2 gets up and jumps up and down on them. Child 1 registers something akin to a pleasure remembered and joins Child 2. They both jump and giggle for a while and then run off to pursue other activities individually.

2. A 7-year-old is part of a directed activity which has resulted in the production of a 'sausage' of shortbread dough. The teacher has set the child the task of making an even number of biscuits from the dough and the child is now trying to decide where to begin. First, he decides that knowing how long the 'sausage' dough is will help: he (inappropriately) choose spans, finds it is one and half and immediately says 'That's too big!' meaning, in this context, his chosen arbitrary measure. He looks at his hands, smiles briefly to himself and proceeds to measure placing finger by finger side by side along the dough. He measures to 15 fingers says out loud 'What's half of 15?', and almost in the same breath says 'Oh, it won't go in half!', at which point he stretches the dough just a little, re-measures and, with great satisfaction, discovers he can now fit in 16 fingers. He then says (using appropriate halving actions) '16, 8, 4, 2, 1 – I can make 16 biscuits!'

Having given some fairly clear, if not extensive, classifications of play in Chapter 1, in this chapter I begin by arguing about them! For the main problem in attempting to discuss play and learning is that the first difficult task, as suggested by Lewis (1982), is that of distinguishing between *play* and *play behaviours*: that which is, in the former case, internal, affective and natural and that which is, in the second case, manifested by the child or adult outwardly. Play, in this latter description, could be considered as process, whereas play in the former might conceivably be seen, as suggested by Bruner (1977, quoted in Chapter 1) and Schwartzman (1982) as a mode. She feels, however, that play is either process or mode: how children and adults regard certain objects or events indicates whether they are, or are not, acting playfully. This can also pertain to attitudes held towards events, activities and other people. The implication is, therefore, that the two are interchangeable. Anything can be playfully undertaken, whatever 'category' or level of activity is involved and it is possible that adults and children switch within the same situations, from being playful to earnest, and back again. More importantly, this may or may not be obvious to an observer. Fortunately for classroom adults it is usually evident with young children.

As an example, is every child who exhibits play as in the first scenario above, affected as inwardly by the experience as the predominant outward behaviour suggests? Is one of the children more motivated by it than the other? What are the children really doing? Are they learning anything? Is that learning useful? Does that kind of play serve any acceptable purpose in school? Did play cease to be such at any time? Readers may contend that children and adults have verbal expressions in order to explain 'activity' in both the affective and cognitive domains and, therefore, a verbal exploration of the above would answer all these questions. Agreed, except how many children do any of us know between the ages of 4 and 8 years who can really competently explore and describe their own feelings and behaviours in words? For the matter, how many adults can do so: for different reasons they are often bound by many recognized and unrecognized constraints from really expressing what they feel about something and describing their own actions.

Particularly in school, it is unlikely according to such writers as Tizard and Hughes (1984), that children can express themselves, because of temporal and interpersonal constraints, as competently, consistently and openly as they do at home. Other problems manifest themselves for teachers when they begin to try to assess what the child is actually *learning* from this exhibited play behaviour. Tizard and Hughes make the additional point that children busy with an activity can rarely participate in intellectually challenging conversations because their attention is directed to the task (1984:261). Teachers have to infer from their outward attitudes, concentration, facial expressions, apparent motivation, and so on, what children's learning is likely to be; otherwise how do they know what teaching and learning is required? As Hyland (1984:29) suggests of analysing one's own play:

The choices of ... play opportunities which we usually make unreflec-
tively can, if reflected upon, be psychologically informative about
ourselves and can raise a set of issues about the psychological significance of these choices that are thought-provoking in themselves.

In the context of the present model, time to explore needs to be set
aside, and the time to talk about and extend learning comes in directed
play. The opportunity for assessing children's responses, understandings
and misunderstandings presents itself in the more relaxed second bout of
free play.

By virtue of the present stance on play, it must now be said that the type
of free play and directed play described in Chapter 1 constitutes both
mode and process, but this needs refining in an attempt to relate these now
to learning. Therefore, the view taken will be basically that the first free
play activities with materials falls within Hutt's (1966) domain of
exploratory play. Directed play is concerned mainly with process. The
second free play situation subsumes process and mode and it is within this
type of play that teachers should look for real learning. However, because
it can transfer itself at any time in any place, herein lies the difficulty. But
this is also where carefully conceived teaching around children's interests
can help planning, thinking, monitoring and assessing (Chapters 6–8 will
explore these issues further). One of the main features of this current
exposition is that it is not in directing the play or in making the decision
about what to direct or how to direct it which will evidence the most
learning. Rather, it is in the opportunity provided to the children to apply
something from the directed play activity to another situation. Hans
(1981:5) explains his thoughts clearly on this aspect when he says 'play as
an activity is constantly generating new situations. It does not merely play
with and within the old ones.' With young children, incidences of learning
can be very small but it is these which take the child a stage or stages
further in learning. And it is these which, freed from the constraints of
either teaching or explicit learning, may truly be regarded as play, for as
Sutton-Smith (1986:145) says: 'Exploration tends to precede mastery
which tends to precede play and they are not always easily distinguish-
able.' Through free, exploratory play, children learn something about
situations, people, attitudes and responses, materials, properties, textures,
structures, visual, auditory and kinesthetic attributes, dependent upon the
play activity. Through directed play, they are proposed another dimension and a further range of possibilities extending to a relative mastery
within that area or activity. Through subsequent extended free play
activities children are likely to be able to enhance, enrich and manifest
learning. The younger the child the more exploratory play is likely to be
needed, but this will be relative to the general background and intelligence
of the child; we must accept that certain children will have had wide-

Plate 4. Incidences of learning can be very small but it is these which take the child a stage or stages further in learning.

ranging exploratory play in their pre-school experiences either at home or in playgroups. They will then come to school with possibly very different expectations of 'play'.

In fact, all children soon become aware themselves that certain play behaviours are inappropriate to the school context, for example the kind of shouting and bellowing one hears emanating from playgrounds within local parks would not (and indeed should not) be tolerated within the school context.

Sceptics might ask, could we not just leave it to the children to use the materials and situations effectively? Surely children learn anyway by just playing? Hans (1981:183) takes up this question when he asks:

how do we learn to play well? ... one direction says that we play well as a matter of course, that it does indeed come naturally to us; the other says that we have all along somehow managed to resist the tendency to play well because it involves us in processes beyond our control [values, risks, perspectives].

All those who have ever watched or been involved in children's play for any sustained period will realize immediately that children do not always provide themselves with such a wide variety of play materials and activities as it is often suggested they do. Sometimes they are quite restricted with resources, manipulating them within a narrow range of potential possibilities, and need prompting to use them in other ways and for other purposes. In the introduction to this book, the suggestion was made that we all view appropriateness differently with regard to different situations. In the context of school it may be that, because of previous suggestions absorbed rightly or wrongly by the children, they feel that certain uses (and abuses) of a range of resources are inappropriate. Consider the 6-year-old child who told me that she was not allowed to make pictures with attribute blocks because they were for 'doing shapes', or the 7-year-olds reintroduced to the water tray after an 18-month gap, who, when asked a question pertaining to what they were learning from their activity, said they were not supposed to learn anything from their forays into the water bath as the teacher had said they were to 'just play'.

We must now turn to what is meant by learning and explore some of the possible theories on learning which fit into the present proposals in regard to play.

Theories of learning

Many psychologists over the years have attempted theories of learning which differ not only in their basic model but stem from very different foci. Claxton (1984) identifies these as cognitive, behavioural, social/personal and humanistic and suggests that, despite very disparate origins, there has now been an intermingling of the different traditions as realization has dawned that there is no one model of learning in relation to all individuals. In any model, learning can only be assessed in terms of what manifests itself externally. This classic view of learning known to many teachers survives in the notion that learning brings about a change of *behaviour* – in the fullest sense of the word. What can be seen to change is that through which learning may be judged. Change can be overt as in some kind of physical response or may be a change in attitude, notoriously more difficult to recognize or assess. If it can be judged it can also be valued, or rather, have values attached to it. We all learn all the time. Our constant state of 'playfulness' according to Hyland (1984) determines this.

Herein lies a major strength of play: individuals, whether adult or child, can play in their own way, drawing from that experience whatever learning they are 'ready' for at that time.

It seems clear in observing children, particularly as in the second scenario above, that there is much more motivation and satisfaction in learning through this type of situation as children can base new learning on what is already familiar and, therefore, it comes more naturally to them. Hans (1981) is quite clear in his own mind that what adults and children elect to formulate in their play and what they learn from it is governed by experience. He asserts:

> Playful choices have nothing to do with chance. When we fall back upon the playful we fall back upon the understanding we always rely on ... falling back on the playful is falling back on what we know best. (Hans, 1981:185)

This stage of 'knowing' in essence gives young children the confidence to want to know more. For as Claxton (1984:216) suggests, 'Learning is essentially a growth, not an accumulation, and it must always spring from and return to what is known.' He later says of the learner:

> Good learners take their time, don't mind asking questions, aren't afraid of saying 'I don't know' or of being wrong, can change their minds and enjoy finding out. (Claxton, 1984:219)

Learning needs and the role of the teacher

Young children often show all of these characteristics and more in their play. Play as process and mode provides a 'learning ethos' in which children's basic learning *needs* can be met. These needs include the opportunity:

- to practise, choose, persevere, imitate, imagine, master, gain competence and confidence;
- to acquire new knowledge, skills, coherent and logical thinking and understandings;
- to be given opportunities for creating, observing, experimenting, moving, cooperating, sensing, thinking, memorizing and remembering;
- to communicate, question, interact with others and be part of a wider social experience in which flexibility, tolerance and self-discipline are vital;
- to know and value oneself and one's own strengths and understand personal limitations; and
- to be active within a safe and secure environment which encourages and consolidates the development of social norms and values.

'Open' play, that which we might call the true play situation, presents a realm of possibilities for children, fulfilling their learning needs and making their explicit learning more overt. Part of the teacher's job is to provide free and directed play situations in which to try to meet children's learning needs and, in this role, the teacher could be called an initiator and enabler of learning. However, by far the most important role for the teacher is that which is undertaken in the third part of the play cycle when he or she must try to decide what the child has learned – the enquirer and assessor role – to be followed by both sustaining and enhancing this learning and returning to the initiator role in the new cycle. This apparently very complex procedure is undertaken in many classrooms serving the needs of the youngest children all over the country at some level or another. Both initial and in-service training must ensure that teachers gain even greater competence in this area in order to keep pace with national trends and sustain the vital role of play in the development of children.

Many very eminent educationalists have concluded that the most valuable learning comes through play (Isaacs, 1930; Schiller, 1954; DES 1967; Lee, 1977; Sylva, 1977; Yardley, 1984; Curtis, 1986) and have supported this by statements such as:

> Play is the child's main business in life; through play he learns the skills to survive and finds some pattern in the confusing world into which he was born. (Lee, 1977:340)

> play is the principal means of learning in early childhood ... children gradually develop concepts of causal relationships, the power to discriminate, to make judgements, to analyse and synthesize, to imagine and to formulate. (DES, 1967: para. 523)

What must always be remembered, however, is that children can and do learn in other ways than through play and often enjoy doing so. An example would be in listening to a story or working alongside adults making or achieving something. Tizard (1977) feels that this more goal-oriented element of play and learning is often forgotten and even frowned upon by nursery school teachers, yet this is the way children have learned over many centuries. She points out that 'obnoxious as the idea may be to nursery school teachers, there is little evidence that free play with bricks teaches the child more than copying a brick model' (Tizard, 1977:207).

Tizard, however, along with most other early educators, does believe that children's conceptual development depends to a large extent on good, first-hand experiences. Much evidence for this multi-sensory approach exists and has done so from Froebel through McMillans to Piaget and on to Donaldson (1978) and Brierley (1987), and is well documented without repetition here. What is important is to interrogate a basic theory of learning which encompasses particularly what schools and teachers do and can do to enhance learning. A particular theory which gives real substance to this, especially in relation to the present discourse on play, is that of Norman (1978), which will now be explored.

Norman's model of learning

The theory, possibly the only true theory of complex learning in existence, has three different processes which essentially link a learner's present knowledge with new experiences to acquire new learning. These processes Norman calls *accretion, restructuring* and *tuning*. The former two are complementary processes because accretion and restructuring can be seen, as indicated in Fig. 2.1, to both follow and precede each other. 'Tuning' is the process by which the learner begins to adopt automatically what has been learned through accretion and restructuring so that what has been a preoccupation in the early stages of acquisition, such as walking or riding a bike, gradually takes on an automaticity which requires any redundancy to be shed. Young children, through exploratory play, spend a great deal of time in the process of accretion. They accumulate a set of discrete notions about a particular material or activity but, once this becomes familiar, increasingly the child will be able to perceive underlying patterns or concepts and predominantly begin the process of restructuring. This process is then likely to be followed by a new period of accretion, and this cycle is likely to be repeated and operated until a period of tuning emerges in which a new learning experience has been thoroughly acquired and becomes 'automatic'. This period is characterized by a fluency or mastery of these recently acquired concepts or skills.

The similarity of this model to that described in the previous chapter in relation to play is exciting and appears to provide enormous support for this view of play in relation to learning. It can be ascribed to any learning experience, be it that of a child or an adult and, although not prescribing what we must do as teachers to foster learning, according to Bennett *et al.* (1984:24) it provokes the question 'which learning processes do teachers demand of children?' These writers used Norman's model as a basis for reviewing task demands made by teachers on infant children and saw the model as implying four different types of task which make different demands on the learners:

- Incremental tasks: basically those which involve the process of accretion and require imitation or step-by-step reproduction of new procedures.
- Restructuring tasks: children work with mostly familiar materials but are required to construct new ways of looking at problems.
- Enrichment tasks: in essence, the second period of accretion which extends the range of application of the new concepts and skills, rather than adding new ones.

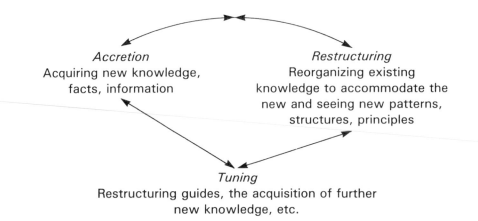

Fig. 2.1. Norman's model of complex learning.

- Practice tasks: repetitive and automatic responses (the process of tuning) and rapid application of familiar knowledge and skills to equally familiar problems and settings (Bennett *et al.*, 1984: 23–4).

To these, Bennett and his colleagues added 'Revision' as, within the classroom setting, they felt that memorizing (or rather 'minimizing the loss of learning') is an important feature. They emphasize that in no way are any of these processes superior or inferior to each other; rather, they make 'qualitatively different demands' (Bennett *et al.*, 1984:26). The amount of time any child spends on any of the five processes will inevitably depend on individual need, but in the context of play, one might expect that relatively equal amounts of time would be likely.

However, the authors, using this model went on to find that practice tasks dominated the school activities of the 6- and 7-year-olds who were the focus of the study and that enrichment and restructuring tasks, those tasks 'demanding discovery or invention, were very rarely presented' (Bennett *et al.*, 1984:29). This is perhaps inevitable where 'work' apparently predominates and supersedes play in respect of teachers' views of learning and their role in making suitable provision.

It appears that this teaching and learning situation described by Bennett and his colleagues – and confirmed by many other sources including the Cockcroft Enquiry into Mathematics (DES, 1982b) and HMI Reports such as the *First School Survey* (DES, 1982a) – could undergo desirable changes if teachers were able to adopt the more play-centred view of learning suggested herein. This, in fact, emphasizes just those elements of learning, i.e. restructuring and enrichment, discovering for oneself and building upon one's own experiences and one's own knowledge to create new concepts and experiences, which appear to be difficult for teachers to provide in a 'work' ethos (Desforges and Cockburn, 1988).

There is another aspect equally worthy of consideration. Revision tasks, as suggested by Bennett *et al.* (1984), are less likely to be required following play because the actual motivation of the concrete experience itself leads to the likelihood of greater memorability to the child (Brierley, 1987:92). Each and every one of us remembers, without a doubt, those things which have been an essential part of our own real experience. We also, as Piaget (1966:vi) pointed out, develop greater understanding generally:

> Children have real understanding only of that which they invent themselves and each time we try to teach them something too quickly we keep them from reinventing it themselves.

Several writers emphasize the importance of learning necessitating building on previous experiences. Connolly and Bruner (1974:310) suggest 'higher skills depend upon the acquisition and orchestrating of previously mastered constituents'. Wagner and Stevenson (1982:203) conclude that learning necessitates knowledge being transferred from task to task and based on wide rather than restricted experiences. Carey (1974:190) argues the case even more strongly when she asserts:

> Because each new skill depends on the last, the effect of unmodularized skills [skills not adequately internalized] is to detract from building new ones.

Doing it 'wrong' as a process of learning

Inevitably, any form or model of learning also implies making mistakes. Many writers have emphasized the importance of making errors in learning. Wells (1985b:18) outlines four recurrent themes in learning, one of which emphasizes 'the value of errors, to learners as elicitors of helpful feedback and, to teachers, as a source of insight into the meanings that their pupils are making'. Bruner (1973:5) suggests that we must all be allowed to be 'fallible' because we learn with such swiftness and can think far beyond the basic information we are given. Saltzberger-Wittenberg *et al.* (1983:58) powerfully support this notion:

> Real learning and discovery can only take place when a state of not knowing can be borne long enough to enable all the data to be gathered by the senses to be taken in and explored until some meaningful pattern emerges.

The child in the second scenario at the beginning of this chapter exemplifies this state of affairs. It is, however, a sad fact that so many learning situations encountered by even very young children in school, accept only correct answers. The page of sums can only be right or wrong and, in this instance, 'wrong' means the child is and feels a failure. Giving names to shapes, word-by-word reading, phonic exercises and filling in template outlines, all emphasize that mistakes are not something to be learned from but *failure!* One of the major features of learning through play must be the opportunity it provides for learning, without threat, from those things which go wrong. The tower building in the first scenario resulted in a good deal of learning about height and stability without any need for ticks and crosses! There was no need for any sense of failure, merely of learning through trial and error. Perhaps teachers sometimes forget how fragile the confidence of a very young child is. Children frequently get out of proportion certain events in school which represent failure and which can result in considerable loss of self-esteem. It is within my experience that many such events do occur in classrooms and frequently result in the unhappy child becoming a passive observer of the home-corner or craft-table inhabitants or spending inordinate amounts of time in the toilet or just quietly sulking. These events can be missed by the busy teacher who has not realized the extent of the unhappiness of the child at his or her apparent failure. Of course, not every child who fails sulks and not every sulker has failed at something. There is also a recognition that children must at some time understand what it is not to achieve success at every turn, but it has equally to be remembered that young children, in the context of school, often need their confidence building to try out the many new ideas and activities presented to them and any sense of failure is unlikely to provide them with the necessary security. However, learning by whatever means should be a stimulating and enjoyable challenge and nowhere more so than in school. It should support the notion of the personal development of the child as a confident, independent individual. It should support the child in knowing who and what he or she is and of that which he or she is capable. (More will be said in Chapter 8 on the issue of children's self-image and personal esteem.)

The incomparable wealth of the child's evident learning within a few short years of life demands our respect. Holt (1975:85–92) warns us not to regard young children as being 'cute' simply because they are naïve lest we become 'incapable of perceiving their behaviour accurately or taking its significance with due seriousness'. Suffice it to say at the present time, the view of play already postulated provides children with a framework which encompasses both trial-and-error learning and has levels of success inbuilt within its parameters.

Motivating and stimulating play

Above all, play motivates. That is why it provides a special climate for learning whether the learners are children or adults. Smith (1982) contends that the motivational aspect of play has and will continue to give it educational value. Play outside school motivates children to explore and experience the home, garden, street, shops, neighbourhood, and so on. It provides a longer time-scale and learning which is likely to be spread out and on-going (Tizard and Hughes, 1984), the developing child being absorbed into the situation at different times and rates according to need. Play within school of necessity motivates different learning and is characterized by greater fragmentation and being compacted into segments of time. This, as teachers, we must accept. We cannot, and indeed should not, try totally to replicate the home situation. The patterns of learning in each situation are likely to be very different although related, and instead of trying to emulate home conditions teachers should not only be attempting to make links for children but also provide them with the necessary *teaching* (for which, after all, all teachers have been trained) which ensures that *learning* takes place! As Sava (1975:14) asserts:

> The important developmental fact is that stimulating children's minds through activities not normally and regularly offered in the home strengthens their cognitive ability to tackle the increasingly difficult learning tasks they will face in the decades ahead.

Dunn and Wooding (1977) feel that the role of adults is central to the development of children's play even when children are later playing by themselves, thus seemingly providing yet more support for the present view of play and the crucial role of the teacher. Children can play freely with building bricks at home: school should be different. It should ensure that children use the variety of experiences outside to learn more within the school context. For as Saltzberger-Wittenberg *et al.* (1983:123) assert:

> The best practices suggest that the good school recognises the importance of the home, does not expect to take the place of parents and accepts that its own role is different but also important.... The children themselves can benefit from recognising that difference, perhaps finding relief in the less intense emotional atmosphere of school, or discovering a new kind of relationship with adults who are not primarily substitute parents and with a group of peers who are not siblings.

Sutton-Smith (1986) feels strongly that, in the toys they buy and present to their children, parents look towards mainly isolated play in the home and that school, therefore, must be expected to provide a major facility for child–child relationships. Blatchford *et al.* (1982:3) produced convincing evidence that young children's relationships with other young children 'have been previously undervalued'. They found that children of the same age interacting together facilitated 'interpersonal discovery and competence' in a way that interactions with socially sophisticated elders did not (1982:154). This interpersonal discovery assists young children in understanding themselves and contributes enormously to personal development. Understanding oneself and gaining confidence in one's own abilities, furthers children's scope for moving towards independence, a feature high on the list of most early educators' aims for young children.

Allied to this, is the physical learning inherent in a young child's play. Balance, control, agility, coordination of eye, brain and muscles combined with manipulative powers over materials, mastery over one's body and competence in one's movements lead to even greater feelings of self-confidence and personal worth. Young children need to move; in fact, they find it almost impossible to stay still and it is easy to believe that they will get all the physical development they need just because of this biological factor. However, much recent evidence has been presented (Wetton, 1988: Ch:3) that young children are not as fit as one would suppose from all this activity and that heart disease and related illness is starting from an earlier age. Teachers must work within the children's capabilities but, in all areas, and particularly physical education, must be prepared to stretch the children's abilities and efforts that bit further in order to gain the desired physical and mental feelings of well-being. Physical activity is exceptionally good for children and adults alike, as it is believed that activity promotes deeper breathing, which ensures that more oxygen is carried in the blood and food is digested and absorbed more readily. Exercise also induces good sleep patterns and adequate rest, ensuring in turn that children are refreshed for a new day, new experiences and new learning!

The words of Stevens (1977) serve to summarize this chapter so far. He says play 'is necessary and vital to "normal" development of both the organism itself and of its maturation as a social being' (1977:242). Learning occurs all the time in normal development throughout life provided something triggers our interest (Sava, 1975:9). Greater potential for future learning from a nursery environment which provides cognitively challenging play has been shown by Jowett and Sylva (1986). The longitudinal study of Osborn and Milbank (1987) concludes that investment in pre-school education, and by earlier inference the quality of the play and learning opportunities within different provisions, could well pay good dividends in the shape of calculable beneficial effects on the children's educational attainments five years hence and perhaps into the longer future. Piers and Landau (1980) report on a study by Feitelson undertaken with matched pairs of Israeli children, half of whom undertook directed play with puzzles, mosaics and blocks and half of whom were tutored on pre-reading skills through pencil-and-paper activities. In a

Plate 5. Teachers must be prepared to stretch the children's ability and efforts that bit further in order to gain the desired physical and mental feelings of well-being.

follow-up test for which they were asked to copy a five-word sentence, the children who had had the opportunity to play made significantly fewer mistakes and approached the task more readily and enthusiastically than did the pencil-and-paper task children. Feitelson concludes that certain types of play may well be more effective in developing the kind of school learning teachers wish to promote than trying to teach the skills directly. The kind of directed play currently advocated appears to gain support from this type of study.

The role of the teacher is to ensure that, in the school context, learning is on-going and developmental in itself and encompasses factors in addition to the purely intellectual. The emotional, social, physical, aesthetic and moral combine with the intellectual to incorporate a total construct of 'learning'. Each is interdependent and interrelated to produce a rational, divergent thinking person who has powers of problem solving and questioning in an infinite variety of situations and performances. The level of such operation is, of course, dependent upon age/stage relationships of development and experience. In the years 4–8, and in the school learning context, particular emphasis needs to be placed on the children's:

1. Active participation in all learning experiences designed to encourage use of all the senses including movement.
2. Opportunities to be introduced to new learning situations and, most importantly, be given the opportunity to restructure existing knowledge and transfer inherent skills and knowledge to new situations and problems in order to find solutions.
3. Opportunities for personal discovery and creativity supported by adults which will lead to the learning of independence of thought and action.
4. Interaction with other children and adults through which to learn a variety of social skills, morals and values.
5. Engagement in meaningful and constructive play situations which will allow development as in (2) above, combined with experience of a wide variety of materials and resources through which to learn.
6. Opportunities to practice and revise skills in a consistent and stable environment and learn without fear of failure.

For certain skills and processes, children may also require the opportunity to learn from good adult models. Part Two will dwell in detail on the type of curriculum which will incorporate optimum learning within the present view of play.

Children also need opportunity for a plethora of talk and purposive discussion with adults and other children about a whole range of personal and environmental issues as well as the language requirements of school and formal learning. These issues are now addressed in Chapter 3.

PART TWO

3

Play Through and with Language

Scenarios

1. Two 6-year-olds are involved in experiments in the water tray which today has detergent added. They have different sized plastic bottles, jugs, funnels and a large plastic straw. One child is pouring the bubbly water through a funnel into a bottle and accumulating a good deal of froth in the funnel. The other child has the straw inserted into his plastic bottle and is producing a torrent of bubbles out of the bottle from the results of blowing through the tubing. Their conversation develops a whole range of topics including the formation of clouds (equated with the bubbles emerging from the top of the bottle), Superman (because he flies through the clouds), rain from the fact that when the bubbles pop they wet the children's faces, the 'disappearance' of items under the opaque bubbly surface of the water and the level the bubbles come up the children's arms as they plunge them into the water. Just as the children's conversation is evolving into a jointly produced story about Superman's adventures in the clouds, the teacher intervenes:

Teacher: What's making the bubbles?
Child 1: Jonathan's being silly! [pokes the straw at him]
Teacher: Jonathan's being silly is he?
Child 2: He's being silly, too! [pushes other child]
Teacher: That's a bit silly! What's making all those bubbles?
Child 2: [giggling] The straw!
Child 1: [giggling] The bubbles!
Teacher: Is the straw making all those bubbles? Are you sure?
Child 1: [holding head down] Straw!
Teacher: Can you think of anything else which might make bubbles?

A long pause ensues.

Child 2: [shaking the bottle vigorously and making a mass of bubbles inside] The bottle.
Teacher: Come on now – think hard!
Child 2: Superman!

The children flick bubbles at each other, are reprimanded by the teacher. The teacher goes away and the children leave the water tray.

2. Three 4-year-olds in a nursery class are playing with Sticklebricks:

Child 1: [to adult] I made a monster!
Child 2: Look at *my* monster!
Adult: Well, they're certainly very frightening!
Child 3: Mine's an Oozy-Woozy monster!
Child 2: So's mine! [All three children and the adult laugh]

There is a short pause, while a few additional features are added to the monsters by the children.

Child 2: It's Loozy-Goozy as well!
Child 3: We've got Oozy-Loozy, Goozy-Foozy monsters!

The monsters are made to collide, and converse with each other in 'oopsy-oozy' vocabulary. The children continue to play with these sounds, laughing at each other's attempts and inviting the adult to join in. The adult declines but continues to be present and watch. Play continues and different faces, hats, feet and other accessories are added and subtracted until Child 1 (who took little part in the earlier conversation) announces:

Child 1: I've made a Nelephant-elephant!

Laughter once more breaks out. The adult offers a few more 'phant' words which children immediately adopt within their play. Play continues for a further 20 minutes (a total of 35 minutes in all) while children explore their rhyming vocabulary.

These two episodes emphasize a number of features which are fairly typical of language interaction in the classroom and school situation. They also lend themselves to a variety of interpretations and analyses which it is the purpose of this chapter to explore.

Children's play episodes frequently involve the use of language as shown in the first example above which might be described as 'words for playing with' (at least before the teacher's intervention, a matter which will be dealt with later). The second describes a scenario which is not so commonly found in school language interactions, that of playing *with* language and words.

What both situations, and others described later, have in common is that they are essentially about children talking and communicating in a meaningful context, for as Halliday (1975) explains:

What is common to every use of language is that it is meaningful, contextualised and, in the broadest sense social; this is brought home very clearly to the child in the course of his day-to-day experience.

But the scenarios do not merely describe children's language use and competence. What they show clearly, particularly in the second example. is the negotiation of *shared* meanings between the participants (Wells, 1985a:21)

Language, communication and shared meaning

Current theories on language development are now clearly emphasizing the communicative aspects of language: language simply cannot occur in a vacuum. It is about the reconstruction of meaning and particularly the construction of shared meanings. For as Wiles (1985:89) suggests:

> Focusing on language rather than content is unproductive. Few people are interested in language for its own sake because language is a tool for communication, not an end in itself.

The communicative aspects of language occur through every aspect of a young child's life and long before entering the world of school or pre-school the child has been part of a language system at home which has emphasized the negotiation of meaning through verbal and non-verbal channels since birth. Studies such as those by Tizard and Hughes (1984) and Wells (1985a, 1986) show plainly that this constitutes far and above the greatest advantage of talk in the home situation, where purposeful language occurs in a natural context and where children themselves initiate language interactions which, in turn, produce more child-oriented and appropriate language use, leading to greater language competence. Wells (1985b) and Hall (1987) both emphasize the purposeful nature of language in community and familial settings for children where adults facilitate children's language learning by responding to them as appropriate language users.

Adults as facilitators, signifies another major feature of language; that, on the whole, children themselves control their own oral language development guided by those around them and aided particularly by children's innate desire to play, particularly with and alongside others. Play situations provide a very appropriate context for language development across both the cognitive and affective domains particularly, as we shall see later, in relation to role play activities.

The strong relationship between play and language is borne out in a study by Levy (1984) wherein she examined a wealth of literature on play and language use in 5-year-olds. She found an 'undeniable association' and concluded that play is an effective medium for stimulating language

Plate 6. Play is an effective medium for stimulating language development and innovation in language use.

development and innovation in language use, particularly in relation to clarifying new words and concepts, motivating language use and practice, developing metalinguistic awareness and encouraging verbal thinking (Levy, 1984:60).

The two examples cited in the scenarios above, indicate just how play and language are interconnected and interactive with each other in the life of the young child. Indeed, language has actually become a play resource in the second example. One could speculate that this playing with words poetically and rhythmically (see Bradley and Bryant, 1985) has developed from earlier experiences of rhymes and children's sheer delight in the sound of unusual or emotive words, e.g. children will read and respond to the words *'Tyrannosaurus rex'*, which brim with mental images of monsters and terror! Meek (1985:46) suggests that:

> By making up words that express feelings children push their imaginative construction of the total scene, of which they themselves are a part, to the boundary of their language and understanding.

The leanings towards storying about the imaginative and mysterious, are also to be found in the first example, though it is unfortunate in this case that this was brought to an abrupt end by the untimely intervention of the teacher! Nevertheless, the potential of children for playing and imagining through words as well as with words can never be under-estimated.

Conversation with a child in a play situation, freed from any aspect of adult 'interrogation', can give deep insights into a child's thinking – and what we as adults are up against when we delve into that domain! A linguistically able young 4-year-old was involved in speculation with me one day after the death of the pet hamster:

Child: Mrs M ... it must be horrible living in heaven.
Mrs M: Now I wonder why you say that?
Child: Well, heaven is in the clouds, isn't it, and you said that the clouds make rain and are full of water, so Sugar will get very wet!

The egocentric speech described by Piaget (1926), which he thought took little account of another's perspectives, must be seriously questioned in the light of this.

Unfortunately, and conversely, young children cannot always find the words to express what they are actually capable of exploring through their internal and personal development of language and thought. A child's ability to verbalize directly to an adult, can rarely be used as an indicator of learning: yet it is so often expected within school that this will happen. By being part of a play situation in which children play with and through language, adults can obtain intriguing insights into children's develop-ment of thinking and learning. The non-verbal dimension of such assess-ment is also worth remembering. The body language associated with the classroom is a fascinating and insightful topic too lengthy to attempt in this short discourse on language and play. Yet it is worth mentioning, because language, in all its forms and contexts, including that of play, provides a vehicle for learning in every sense of the word.

Young children learn language: sometimes more than one language. They also learn *through* language. But they also reason and communicate *with* language. In the early years, this is more often than not in the context of play. Language is inextricably bound up in thought processes and the development of mental images. While several eminent thinkers, such as Piaget, Bruner, Chomsky and Vygotsky, have postulated different theories of the relationship between language and thought and sought to answer the chicken-and-egg situation of which comes first within the developing child, an absolute solution has remained elusive and will, no doubt, continue to do so given the enormous complexity of the task. The fact that the two have a deep interrelationship is probably sufficient for the purposes of examining and exploring children's language through and within play situations. That language has a functional importance, that it is a container of thought and that it is also a determinant of thought is not in question. As Hall (1987:73) suggests:

> The learning achieved by young children demands respect. In the almost total absence of explicit instruction, children move from a state of almost complete helplessness to a stage where they are articulate, reasoning human beings, constructing many complex hypotheses about the way the world works.

Nowhere does this occur more so than in the processes and modes of play. The fact that language permeates every aspect of children's lives and education serves only to emphasize its enormity and its all-pervasive nature.

Play and language

All that was said earlier of play in relation to process and mode, plus play and play behaviours apply equally if, for play, one substitutes the word 'language'. Language provides both the means towards, and eventually the manifestation of, learning. Within the processes of the learning spiral postulated in Chapter 1, language is of cardinal importance in providing both a channel for expressing the learning occurring through play and a means of internalizing that learning for future restructuring and enrichment according to Bennett *et al.*'s (1984) model of learning described in Chapter 2. Time to explore children's language must be set aside by teachers, however difficult to arrange for. In directed play, teachers will have the opportunity to extend vocabulary, discuss previous play processes and generally extend children's thinking through discussion and conversation. Opportunities to explore children's responses, under-standings and misunderstandings will occur in the more relaxed atmosphere of the second and subsequent play bouts, when dialogue is likely to be more temporally related and significant.

Because children have also been party to a 'trial-and-error' situation in acquiring and developing their language, and will hopefully continue to do so for many years, the emphasis on learning by exploration and experimentation is also a vital feature of language and play. As part of acquiring semantic and syntactical elements, children often overplay a 'rule' such as 'I goed to school' or 'I saw two mouses'. This is a vital part of language acquisition and, while corrected by adults, is generally considered to be a step in the right direction rather than an error. Wells and Nicholls (1985:18) conclude that:

> the value of errors, to learners as elicitors of helpful feedback and, to teacher, as a source of insight into the meanings that their pupils are

making, is a major recurrent theme in facilitating – or impeding –
pupils' active involvement in language learning.

We must now turn to the teachers' own language interactions with
children and the provision made for learning, to explore these issues
further.

Language, play and the teacher

Many studies, including a recent one by Desforges and Cockburn (1988)
on teaching mathematics to young children, have stressed the overem-
phasis on a teacher's use of language for control rather than for teaching
purposes. Edwards and Mercer (1987) paint a black picture of child-
centred education which is little more than a process of 'cognitive
socialization' in which communication between teacher and children
emphasizes the 'rituals' of learning rather than conceptual understanding
(Edwards and Mercer, 1987:157). However much one would wish to
argue with some of the statements made, those who frequently observe
practice in schools would have to admit to the accuracy of much of what
Edwards and Mercer contend. Teachers *do* teach, often it must be said, to
the detriment of children's learning. Consider in the first scenario which
began this chapter how, in an effort to teach about the properties of air, the
teacher actually destroyed a very purposeful language interaction which
appeared to be the context for very rich language play and meaningful
communication for the children.

One can continue to empathize with teachers in relation to the number
of children with which they inevitably have to deal, but one cannot ignore
the sheer quantity of very valuable research which both espouses
alternatives and offers solutions to logistical and practical difficulties.
Student teachers inevitably feel that children are only learning when they,
the students, are teaching. Given a good deal of experience and many
opportunities for both observing and engaging in children's play, teachers
of many years' standing *still* believe this to be the case. Edwards and
Mercer offer an explanation in saying of learning and of teachers'
transmitting that which is to be learned:

> Part of the problem for pupils is that much of the process remains
> mysterious to them. In however friendly and informal a manner,
> they are frequently asked to do things, learn things, understand
> things, for no apparent reason other than that it is what the teacher
> wants them to do. The goals and purposes of the lesson are not
> revealed. Indeed, often neither are the concepts that the lesson may
> have been designed to 'cover'. (Edwards and Mercer, 1987:158)

This must relate nowhere more emphatically than in the area of language, given an acceptance of the earlier premises that language is essentially communication and the sharing and negotiating of meaning. We must view and treat children as youngsters trying to make sense of the situation in which they find themselves. Hall supports and reiterates this view in writing on literacy:

> there are many teachers in schools who provide experiences of literacy which make sense only in terms of school instructional practices. Those experiences do not represent a rich, meaningful literacy experience for children.... There is little if any relationship between those experiences and the world outside school.... Children's own ideas about literacy are ignored or rejected. (Hall, 1987:173)

The need for play occurs from within the child (Gessell *et al.*, 1973): so does the need for a language to talk with and through. I contend that a way to 'free' the teacher for real, meaningful oral discussion with children is through the provision of context-rich language play as described by Katz (1985), who writes on helping communication skills in early education:

> The evidence suggested by other papers in this issue indicates that young children benefit greatly from play and from interactions with each other and with adults in small informal groups in which their work and other activities are context-enriched and of real interest to them. Those with major responsibility for setting the goals and priorities for early childhood education can contribute much to improving practice by insisting on postponing formal teaching to at least the junior age range for most children. (Katz, 1985:67)

By being part of the learning spiral through play, teachers will not *need* the artificial props of recorded work for the assessment of language development. They will be part of it. We do tend to move children too quickly to the formal recorded word, rather than the spoken, mainly because it gives us visual confirmation of learning from which we can feel some sense of worth and satisfaction. The problem is that we do not really *know* what effect we have on children: this is why 'tangible' evidence such as pages of writing or sums give us some security. This is not to deny that children need encouragement and opportunity to become avid and enthusiastic writers. However, none of this will occur if children are not allowed opportunities through play situations in which to explore scribble writing as a form of communication growing from the spoken word, *and* a perceived need to communicate on paper. For as Hall suggests, in a book full of very readable and worthwhile suggestions on facilitating the emergence of literacy:

Child-centred, play based education should mean that conversation is initiated by the child and taken further by the teacher. However, visits to large numbers of classrooms suggest that at post-nursery level this is rarely the case. (Hall, 1987:16)

Personal experience would lead me to suggest that even at this level it is rare that teachers are using anything but very functional and managerial language with young children, a fact supported by many of the findings of the Oxford Pre-School Research Project of which the writing of Wood *et al.* (1980) forms a part. They uphold adult involvement in children's play and conclude that:

the path to effective interaction lies in a contingent response to the child. Adult language and actions should be keyed in as far as possible to his thoughts and actions, but these can be magnified, developed and extended if the adult is prepared to build on them and expose her own ideas. (Wood *et al.*, 1980:189)

There is no need for a long list of play and language activities for which teachers should make provision. Most teachers are skilled in providing activities for children's language and literacy development and many useful books, such as *Bright Ideas for Language Development* (1984) exist. Basically, it is a question of taking play activities seriously and treating children engaged in play seriously and with respect. The following suggestions are aimed at encouraging readers to contemplate language within their provision of play opportunities for children. They represent those areas to which I feel insufficient attention is given in classes, especially for the 5- to 8-year-olds where play provision is sometimes not used to its greatest effect or potential. The topics are of necessity limited and intended only to supplement, reinforce and, occasionally, reinform as well as provide a new slant for thinking about language and play.

Valuing communication

Teachers must truly value children's communication in the classroom context, not just those occasions when children are responding to the teacher but when children are exploring ideas and mental images of their own through personal and individual dialogue with the teacher or with other children. It should always be remembered that, as teachers, we cannot always know about and, therefore, we cannot always operate in tandem and empathy with the feelings children want to explore about certain events of great significance to them. We can ensure that a variety of situations and innovations within the classroom allow different opportunities for different children and, more importantly, that each child is allowed the opportunity to explore a new medium or situation adequately – and that means attempts at exploring things in words as well as through active play. Instances of children engaged in exciting communication with each other abound in collections such as that edited by Clark (1985), but teachers rarely even know these vital conversations are taking place. Yet there is little doubt regarding the richness of children's development of mental images through language which enhance all children's opportunities to learn, but particularly aid those children who have not had so many experiences before coming to school. Is this not why we need nursery education as opposed to the rather diverse provision we have in this country at present, with staff who understand the vital nature of the links between children's first-hand sensory experiences and the development of imagery, language and abstract thought?

Talking about their play situations with adults both values the play itself and provides opportunities for children to develop a sense of purpose, audience and register. We must value play as a child's *culture* which, like any culture, has its own language (Bettleheim, 1981). Like any culture, play can provide its own barriers to 'outsiders', and communication with adults about play may be difficult not only because of the differences in values but also because adults do not belong to this particular culture (even though they once did!).

Valuing play in these ways also means being prepared to *listen*. Teachers are frequently heard complaining about the fact that children now seem less able to listen than they once were. Although there is no research evidence for this, it could well be so given the constant background noise from television, radio, stereos, computers, and so on, but teachers also need to give thought to the fact that they themselves, for a multiplicity of reasons, are not always good at listening. In the rush and bustle of the classroom, attempting to fit in all curriculum requirements, we tend to rush children, to finish sentences for them, to intervene when a moment's pause would have indicated a need for quiet (an example would be that given in Scenario 1 above), to delay conversation with a child in order to reprimand another – the list could be endless. But as Wells (1985b:33) suggests:

> To be a careful and sympathetic listener and respond to the meaning intended by the speaker are qualities that characterize the behaviours of conversationalists of any age … particularly important when interacting with a much less adept conversational partner.

What we must also ensure is that children feel our communication is directed at them personally. We all know the 'you-must-be-talking-to-someone-else' syndrome! Whole class discussions cannot, with all the available strategies, be directed at individuals. Therefore, time must be made for small group discussions and occasional individual talk with children. We all know and recognize that some children need a good deal more time than others in order to communicate effectively and we must consider that, perhaps for these children, individual conversation is even more vital. Katz (1985) reports unpublished research by Crahay in 1980 which has shown that within a typical pre-school class only about five or six of the children (those who are most articulate) are receiving most of the teacher's verbal interaction, suggesting that teachers tend to engage in greater amounts of interaction with those children who have the greatest verbal fluency and ability. No one would deny that these children need their talk and communication valued, but these are just the children who could be encouraged toward group discussion, particularly within play situations without the constant supervision of the teacher.

Questions and questioning

If teachers are to value children's talk, one serious factor must be considered and that is the asking of questions. In the 'normal' world outside school it is the children who ask all the questions: not so in school! Certain types of questions are essential in order to promote children's thinking but teachers would be well advised to tape themselves during classroom exchanges (Tough, 1977b). Wood and Wood (1983:160) emphasize 'The way a teacher talks to young children helps to determine how active, forthcoming and competent they may appear.' At around the age of 4 or 5 particularly, children ask for confirmation of events and experiences through the questions they ask. This is their way of beginning to sort out fantasy and reality and actually heralds a new period of autonomy in the child's ability to cope with the world. It enables children to create imaginary situations in language and in play. Yet so many of the teacher's questions involve very brief, often functional, answers, or clearly are seeking answers the teacher already knows and which the children know the teacher knows (interrogation)! Frequently, this has the opposite effect to what most people believe, in that it actually makes the child or person to whom the question is directed feel intimidated and defensive, rather than creative and imaginative. As Wood and Wood (1983:162) suggest: 'He who questions, controls!' Again, the 'right/wrong' syndrome prevails: if teachers already have a predetermined answer in their heads the children can only be right or wrong and they know it!

Play, language and children from different ethnic backgrounds

If we deny children a pride in their own use of language or languages they have learned before coming to school, this will have tremendous detrimental effects on their whole attitude to school, learning and ultimately life-skills in general. Blatchford *et al.* (1982) talk of the 'parallel worlds' of home and school and comment that this:

> can lead to missed opportunities; it means that a potentially valuable cooperation is not set in motion – one that would benefit the child, because he would expand his horizons by bringing aspects of the two environments in relation to each other. (Blatchford *et al.*, 1982:164)

This, of course, applies particularly to children for whom English is a second or even third language. It is now well-documented and recognized that well-developed competence in the use of a first language, has enormous implications for the effective learning of a second language (Cummins, 1982; Saunders, 1982). All languages have a structure which, once mastered, helps in the acquisition of other languages. Children need many examples of all languages being used, and *valued*, to begin to construct their own models of language (Nord, 1980). Receptive language needs time to develop and, therefore, moments of silence, of standing watching others in play and communication situations may persist in second language learners, or indeed in reluctant or very young first language learners. Expressive language takes even more time and, because language is so tied up in culture, many experiences need to be provided for children before they begin to make adequate associations. What we must remember is that children speak more freely to other children, even those who speak a different language. There is the commonality of being children. As Coates (1985) asserts:

> Groups of children interacting informally in structured environments can often help the child ... to develop his linguistic skill, as the simple directness of the questions and explanations make immediate rapport possible.

It is vital that children remain in the classroom context to learn English, to have extra language tuition or indeed be part of mother-tongue teaching (The Swann Report: DES, 1985b). Any other arrangement is socially and culturally divisive: in learning a language, one also adopts the cultural perspectives 'hidden' within its framework and this can be supplied by other children and adults who are part of the normal classroom environment. It is vital too that parents from different cultures and ethnic backgrounds are invited in to tell stories and rhymes as well as to help children generally. Some of the best language moments in my own classroom experience have come from sampling the results of a parent's special cooking activity with the children.

Clearly, visual support is also needed in order for children to succeed in tasks requiring them to use another language: puppets, toys, models, a 'story-bag' with items inside which link in some way with the story to be told or read, items of clothing which different people in a story may wear and, of course, pictures. Collaborative play situations across cultures and gender, such as play in the home corner or variations of this pretend play situation, where different cultural media are added, supplements the variety of language used and values the diversity of cultures from which children emanate. A collection of different types of clothing, multi-ethnic dolls, different cooking utensils and pottery, serving dishes, eating implements and different types of furniture arrangements and decoration all add new dimensions to an existing play situation.

Much more could, and perhaps should, be said regarding mother-tongue teaching and learning and some aspects will be considered further in Chapter 9. However, interested readers would be well advised to read more specialized texts such as Edwards (1983), Houlton (1985), Houlton and Willey (1985) and Arnberg (1987).

Play with language

The work of the Opie's (1959, 1969) gives ample evidence of children's delight in playing with language. The second scenario above gives a short example in the school context. More opportunities need to be made for this imaginative use of language. Poems such as the 'Jabberwocky' by Lewis Carroll and those by Michael Rosen delight even the youngest children. It does not matter that they do not understand the words; hearing them is what is important. Being then allowed to play with them is vital. Children do this when they are given the opportunity of 're-reading' a familiar book: the words they use are similar to the original but have the child's very own variations placed on them. These need not be corrected but can be discussed with the child and alternatives explored. As Hall (1987:91) asserts: 'Children should never need to ask if they can engage in purposeful literacy acts.'

Playing with language helps children to understand sense and nonsense and this becomes apparent at the top infant level where children develop a quite acute sense of the ridiculous and 'knock-knock' jokes abound. To deny children this play with language would be disastrous, so why not make it legitimate for them? Provide them with monster puppets, allow them to make extraordinary machines with junk, encourage them to model funny characters and then, all importantly, initiate some strange or humorous nonsense words of your own and then let the children do the rest. If one has classroom animals or a pets' day occasionally, they provide a rich source of possible plays with words, as given a little stimulation, children will delight in making up things for the animals to say – and funny voices in which to say them! All young children enjoy the humour of funny and unusual words and many adults continue to enjoy this kind of word play and play on words themselves. Writers who retain something of this sense/nonsense dimension are often the ones some of us return to for relief from the pressures of the world, such as Tom Sharpe and Spike Milligan. Children enjoy the familiarity of nursery rhymes, humorous poems, television jingles and comic characters and, similarly, retreat to them occasionally for comfort and security. Why do we not allow them more opportunity to do this in the school setting?

The pre-sleep monologues of young children researched by Weir (1962) show clearly how young children spend a good deal of time before sleeping in playing with words and sounds, apparently systematically trying out sound and word combinations. Her young son built up and then broke down again grammatical rules without the conventions of conversation intervening and clearly enjoyed and sustained the process over many weeks, and months.

Rosen and Rosen (1973) are of the opinion that we must promote children's playing with words in ways we have perhaps not encouraged sufficiently before. They suggest that there is ample evidence that children must be motivated to use their own vocabulary forms as this inventiveness in children's speech is of vital importance to future language competence. Meek (1985:47) suggests that children understanding 'nonsenses' in words have first to recognize what she calls 'the language of common sense' and this is a major step in language and cognitive development.

Our provision for play then should legitimize word play and make the notion of words fun rather than the more serious and less purposeful role it has sometimes exhibited in school. Let the children see that *you* enjoy words and comic language structures, let children question you about what you say and even correct you when you get it 'wrong'. Try saying 'I've got two mouses' to a class of 6-year-olds and listen to their responses. This opens up a whole new dimension for talking about language and about the rules which govern speech and the communication of meanings.

Play through language

Children use language in their play most of the time, even talking to themselves or to toys and playthings! A particular, and sometimes underrated context for the development of language, communication skills and competence, is in the area of pretend play which is often accompanied by complex language interactions. 'The play inaugurates, discusses, elaborates and promotes the imaginary and the metaphorical' according to Meek (1985:50). Pretend play provides children not only with the opportunity to begin where they currently 'are' but to use their real and imaginary experiences for language and learning. All children delight in donning the apparel and imagined role of another, particularly those characters from the adult world whom they attempt to understand through their emulation. Exploring the evidence of studies such as those by Smith (1977) and Fein (1981), Chazan *et al.* (1987:62) conclude that: 'pretend play does seem to be related to an increase in divergent thinking skills ... verbal fluency and story-telling skills'. Pretend play is also the successor to dramatic role play which, according to Hutchcroft (1981:209) 'represents a way of organising experience by creating a heightened awareness through play of language and gesture'. Equally Smith (1988:109) believes that 'the ability to fantasize or pretend is, like early language and like the recognition of self, a basic component of the symbolic activity of the child' and he goes on to suggest that the structural development of both are very closely linked.

Sometimes, pretend play, particularly involving the use of language to explore the concepts and established images created within the child, can help children to learn about something without experiencing it for themselves, for example that fire burns. Turning the home corner into the Three Bears' Cottage can help children to experience what it might be like to be frightened and alone as well as providing rich opportunities for comparative language. The provision at other times of three different sizes of towel or blanket, particularly if they are sometimes striped, at other times spotted, different colours, fringed and not fringed, etc., provides a wealth of both language opportunities and the creation of an ideal situation for directed play – 'Today, teddy has whispered to me that he would like this large, fringed towel, and his red and white striped blanket.' With a little of this type of direction, children will quickly begin to develop ideas for themselves about what might be best in the home corner today and will direct each other, particularly if other things around them in the classroom such as a particular colour area become a focus of their attention. Selection might also be dependent upon what role they are adopting within the situation.

On other occasions, role play will be encouraged by the home corner becoming one of the following:

- a castle
- a space station
- an animal home
- a lighthouse
- different kinds of tent
- an aeroplane, vehicle or ship's interior
- a snow den
- a kitchen or other specific room in the house
- a recording studio for radio and TV programmes
- a guest house or hotel
- a museum
- a cave
- an under-the-sea realm

- a caravan
- a boat
- a classroom for the dolls
- a greenhouse
- a stable or a farm
- an artist's studio
- a palace
- a hospital or doctor's surgery

Instead of these (or preferably in addition to them), the teacher can initiate a wealth of imaginative role play in the provision of shops, not just the well-used empty packet, grocery shop but a range of excellent alternatives such as:

- a post office
- a hats and gloves shop
- a tie shop
- a bank or building society
- a second-hand swap shop
- a newsagents and bookshop
- a café, restaurant or tea-shop
- a seaside shop
- a McDonalds' or 'Wimpys'
- a shoe and handbag shop
- a clothes shop
- a hairdresser's
- a ribbons and braids shop
- a button and fastening shop
- shops to sell toys, sweets cakes and bread
- a greengrocer's
- a garden shop
- an ironmonger's
- a supermarket
- a travel agents
- a citizen's advice bureau
- a record and tape shop
- a fishmonger – real, wet fish has true sensory properties!
- a wallpaper shop (children having made their own rolls of printed wallpaper – with matching fabrics!)
- a perfumery or even a chemist (with care as to what children bring in!)
- a computer shop (children can make keyboards and many other items with junk materials, as well as having the real thing around)
- a repair shop for electrical goods (old ones, of course!)

- a baby shop (all children love going back in time and bringing in things from their own earlier childhood)

(All retail type shops carry the opportunity for a sale!).

None of these has to be elaborate or even convincing – to adults. Children bring the power of imagination to bear very fruitfully. There will, of course, need to be the opportunity for free play with these new and exciting 'areas' but then, vitally, they will need teacher direction if they are to explore other dimensions with other learning. These kinds of role play situations provide almost the perfect environment both for play and language as well as a thoroughly integrated approach to the curriculum.

Resource provision for role play needs to be very carefully considered. A home corner or shop which remains the same for several weeks is unlikely to forward a child's experience past the first cycle of free and directed play modes. What is required is imagination and a little time for development and adaptation as play proceeds. As Coates (1985:57) says:

> The preparation of appropriate motivational materials for groups of children selected for their varying language skills and ability to work together, would appear to be important at this beginning stage of education offering the opportunity for language to grow, develop and have meaning.

The promotion of social play, however important, should not cloud the fact that we do not all like to be part of a group all of the time. Children, like adults, enjoy moments of quiet within which they can reflect or exercise their own judgements. Many such moments can be found of solitary play within imaginative role play situations. The language of the solitary child, where he or she constitutes both parties to the discourse, can give immense insights into a child's thinking to a perceptive and quietly observing adult. These moments should be cherished by the adult just as they are by the child.

To conclude this short section, it is worth recording a view of Sutton-Smith (1986), who feels strongly that toys actually encourage solitary play where little overt language is likely to be encountered and certainly no social language. Anyone who has watched children deeply absorbed with constructional toys or water play or in manipulating the events in the doll's house, will immediately recognize that this solitary kind of play does occur in the classroom. What it is worth remembering is that for many young children this is also the main kind of play which occurs in the home environment. Perhaps we should be encouraging more social play in the school context; certainly, imaginative role play in the contexts described above would offer more opportunities.

Play about language

The story method of reading is really a form of word and picture play and is an immediately pleasurable activity for children and adults alike as well as providing a rich source for imaginative functioning. According to Meek (1985:42), children's earliest encounters with books and print are of paramount importance to them but even more important is how teachers talk to children about reading and about how this is interpreted by the children. It is through books that children will begin to learn something about metalinguistics, the language of language, the notion of words, sentences, pages, letters, full stops, commas, speech marks, paragraphs and the like. In addition, the Kingman Report (DES, 1988a) recommends within its attainment targets that children at the age of 7 should be able to 'Use and understand such simple terms of description as are necessary when discussing their language with teachers', and gives examples of children discussing words and substitute words for different purposes and audiences. Some children come to school with the incalculable benefit of being able to reflect on what is said to them. Others will need a great deal of time, experiences and effort to learn to say what they mean and explore their thoughts in language and about language. The Report of the Kingman Inquiry into English Teaching (DES 1988a) epitomizes these notions, suggesting that children must learn to use words other than nouns, give and receive instructions, use different tenses, complex sentences, sentences relating to cause and effect and be able to paraphrase the speech of others.

Reading to children with appropriate intonation and stress helps them to understand the meaning of words (Dombey, 1983), the shared experience of pleasure making it memorable! Re-reading stories fits well into the play spiral as words are enhanced and explored over and over again gradually building on meanings. Children within the story approach appear to move from speech discourse (interactive language) to text discourse (reading) fairly smoothly as the association with voice, tone, stress, intonations and so on is made early. The evidence is available for all to hear when a child 'reads' a big book following exactly the same language conventions as the teacher. Opportunities need to be provided for children to play at being the teacher and enjoying a story or poem with a group of peers. As Brierley (1987:52) suggests: 'By explaining, selecting, or simply recounting, knowledge becomes rooted in thought and language instead of possessing but a frail hold.'

Writing is an equally vital area of literacy development and learning about language. It was thought, in the past, that writing skills lagged behind reading skills by several months, but recent research (Hall, 1987) and the National Writing Project accounts suggest that in fact this was the effect of delayed opportunities for experimental writing rather than a delayed ability. It should be as natural for children to engage in purposeful scribbles as in purposeful reading. The suggestions made above in regard to role play are prime situations in which to introduce children to writing for writing's sake as well as for a real purpose. A café in the classroom with all requisite materials for café 'play' including a note pad for collecting orders, inspires real writing, and it is surprising how much accuracy children show (although this is not, of course, the important factor). Class or school newspapers or newsheets, particularly using the variety of computer word-processing facilities now available, such as Front Page and Folio, encourage even the youngest children to attempt to write at least a few words and, more importantly, to see the processes of drafting and redrafting before final presentation.

Final remarks

In relation to the play spiral, exploring language, playing with language and using language for play are vital. The fact that children may also learn about language is a bonus. This is more likely to occur if adults involve themselves in play and provide a model for children. One student who kept a superb logbook of her teaching practice experience with photographs and records of her children's pictures and written activities, was quite perturbed one day when she found the children avidly 'reading' her tome. But she had, in fact, done exactly the right thing. In poring over her logbook she had represented to the children the behaviour of a literate adult and children, in effect, modelled themselves on this behaviour. Class timetables, too, are an integral part of the world of words and should be shared with children.

From the teacher's point of view the exploratory language play is likely to occur within whatever activity is provided if children are allowed the opportunity to talk to one another and to a cooperative, listening adult. At this time, children will draw on their own prior experiences of this situation and review language and concepts already formulated. The directed language play is likely to occur when opportunities are given to children to talk about activities and what they understand from and about them, from which the teachers will be able to provide language activities to promote thinking further, extend vocabulary and perhaps begin to talk with children about language. The second bout of free play incorporates that which has been previously learned and, at this stage, children themselves may make suggestions for further materials or resources being provided. This will incorporate enrichment, practice, repetition and revision of what has been learned through language, with language and about language.

This chapter has not been about learning to read or write or even learning to speak, but about truly valuing and using language through play as communication and as shared constructions of meaning. Language, it will be shown in the next chapter, also plays a vital role in children learning to solve problems and think logically.

4
Solving Problems Through Play

Scenarios

1. A 6-year-old is attempting in clay to reconstruct his image of a church which has recently been the subject of an investigation walk within the school's locality. He has already solved the problem of realism by breaking the clay into small shapes which he has termed 'bricks' and building them layer upon layer to get the effect he desires. However, as the structure begins to develop height, the prominent corner wall starts to lean inwards with the sheer weight of the wet clay. After several attempts to keep the corner wall upright by pushing his hand inside, by getting another child to do so, by propping the structure up with a piece of wooden dowling, he suddenly alights upon the idea of buttressing it with a thick wedge of clay which happened earlier to have been cut from the whole pack ready for use. That done, he continues to build his corner wall to a considerable height adding thick clay wedges at opportune moments before disaster strikes.

2. Two 4-year-olds are working together on a model of a rocket made from several boxes stuck one on top of the other. The structure is very unstable and is only standing erect because one child is supporting it while the other one adds boxes. They are using sticky tape, only recently introduced to them as a bonding medium. The adult asks 'Will your rocket stand up on its own?' The children let go and it falls over. The adult asks how they can ensure that it will stand up next time. The answer appears to be more sticky tape! This attempted to no avail, the adult explores with them the idea of a launch pad and directs them to a picture of a rocket launch which is on display. This they discuss together, find more boxes (and more sticky tape) and erect a gantry which they then use to lean their rocket against.

Life constantly presents us all with problems; if only of the 'how-to-pay-the-bills' kind! Life offers less problems to young children in a way because someone else is always there to think for them and thus, in some sense, denying them the need to solve problems for themselves. Yet in their play, one can constantly see at least the germ of children thinking about problems and solutions as has been shown in the two scenarios above. The first, however, is characterized by the child's own need to look for a possible solution; the second by the adult in a sense defining the problem for them. Overtly, children's natural response to a problem is to ask for help, as anyone who has tied many, many pairs of shoes laces will corroborate. The caring nature of those who deal with young children generally means that this is sufficient to produce a response – end of problem!

Yet there is much research evidence accumulating to suggest that the opportunity to play in a variety of ways with a variety of materials is closely linked with the development of both abstract (symbolic) and divergent thinking skills which, in turn, foster problem-solving abilities (Pellegrini, 1985). Pepler (1982) suggests that there are three common themes linking play to problem solving and divergent thinking which are:

- specific exploration providing initial information about objects;
- the experimental and flexible nature of play; and
- symbolic object play which could facilitate the transition from concrete to abstract thinking, the former gaining support from Bruner (1972) and the latter from Vygotsky (1977:76).

This has the appearance of fitting equally neatly into the present play spiral notion and further support is given by Lieberman (1977) and Dansky (1980), the first of whom positively correlated teachers' ratings of children's playfulness to their divergent thinking skills, and the latter who suggests that fantasy/pretend play leads to children being able to offer up more 'alternative-use' possibilities for objects following a period of free play with them than a control group. Smith and Simon (1984:204) agree that such results appear to support the view that there is a general superiority of play over non-play conditions evidenced for divergent tasks, but warn that the methodology of such studies is difficult to accept given the elusive nature of the construct of play, let alone the relative ignorance still existing on the *effects* of play (Smith and Simon, 1984:213).

Notwithstanding this, Vandenberg (1986:117) sees children's play as a potentially valuable natural resource that can be used to develop creative individuals who will be the source of technological innovation so necessary for our economic survival, suggesting the use of children's play as the foundation for meeting society's future demands, demands upon which we can only speculate but which we can be sure will need adaptability and flexibility in large measure.

Having recently worked closely with a group of 5-year-olds attempting to resolve the problems of height and stability, I feel strongly that earlier opportunities for play with a variety of materials enabling the building of tall structures did indeed increase, at the end of a 6-week period, the children's ability to formulate a variety of solutions which they were not able to accommodate in the early stages. What was really significant was that *every* child was able to offer something, occasionally a solo solution but more often than not a group result. This has also been found by Burns (1987), who discovered that teachers undertaking problem-solving activities were made to rethink the whole question of children's intelligence and abilities in the light of their new approach to learning with children. It is sometimes quite rare for the really able children in a class to have their capabilities stretched. Yet these are often the children who cannot only solve problems but can set them in the first place, giving them a role in the class and enabling them to use their talents to the full.

What even very young children are clearly able to do is ask many 'why' questions, which gives some indication that, with a little assistance and encouragement to use albeit limited experiences, there are answers which children can find themselves. This highlights the point made in the previous chapter about who it is who asks the questions in most nursery and infant classrooms. It also stresses the interrelationship between all elements of early childhood education and language which is the chief means through which all of us think, reason and respond. One humorous example highlights an occasional difficulty teachers and children experience. Three 5-year-olds attempted to build a house for a teddy from junk materials. In typical fashion, they constructed what amounted to a perimeter wall, in which they proudly sat teddy and then asked the teacher to come and look at their house. The teacher said that the house looked interesting but added: 'What if it rains? What will happen to teddy?' The children looked puzzled. Then an answer clearly struck one child: 'It can't rain in our classroom, Mrs M!' In setting the children the task of building a house for teddy, the adult clearly had in her mind a representation of a house with walls and a roof. The children evidently had different needs in mind.

There are a number of other features at the heart of being able to set and solve problems which are very natural to young children. As Curtis (1986:94) says: 'Problem solving involves an enquiring mind and a natural curiosity and in this respect children are natural problem solvers.' But being able to solve problems also requires that children recognize them in the first place! From the results of a study into metacognitive awareness, Brown and Campione (1978) showed that, unlike older children and adults, younger children are less aware of what they need to know in order to carry out a task. In effect, this means that in school, the classroom must be viewed as being potentially full of problems to solve of the very smallest kind to a wider perspective and provide a stable structure from which children can explore objects, situations and events. In fact, we all know this to be the case in all classrooms where children learn that all four legs of the chair must be on the table for it to balance, that on book shelves the largest books will usually only fit on the bottom shelf and that if you have only eight pence you will have to decide on something else other than the bag of crisps you really wanted for your lunch! Perhaps adults in the classroom do not give sufficient thought to the room, the needs of its occupants and the problems which it sets. We will also have contemplated at some time or another where to put the 'quiet corner' and established it as far away from the door and the ongoing human traffic as possible, but how often do we share these decisions, or even a recognition of the problem, with the children?

The HMI document *Primary Schools: Some Aspects of Good Practice* (DES, 1987a) suggests that where activities of this type are in evidence, the best practices occur. In one school, a class of 7-year-olds were given a choice from three different places they might visit. After the initial 'We'll go there because I want to' type response, careful guidance on the part of the teacher ensured that a decision was made that the children would list first of all what they wanted from their visit. That complete, in workable friendship groups they then listed what they would need, e.g. toilets, not too long on the coach, shade if it was hot, space to play and a clean place to eat their lunch. A class discussion, using the teacher as notetaker – with a very large sheet of paper – gave evidence of the need for putting all the accumulated information together in some usable form. The teacher introduced the idea of a matrix, prepared some blank format sheets over lunchtime and the children explored what they could do at the start of the afternoon. Many attempts, discussions, free play and directed activity abounded before a decision was finally taken that a local wooded beauty spot followed by a short walk to a nearby park would satisfy all requirements and provide an enjoyable day for everyone. This done, the children then, of course, booked the coaches, interviewed the headteacher in regard to insurance requirements, wrote letters to their parents and generally took charge: they gained perceptibly from the whole activity, as did the teacher, who confessed that she would never have imagined it all possible.

It is clear that any such educational experiences offered to young children should not overload their ability to see clearly what these are all about or their capacity for remembering the essentials (Case, 1982; Chazan *et al.*, 1987:113). The number of items of information presented at any one time must be kept low, something which this particular teacher did most skilfully. Halford (1980) suggests that children aged 5–11 years can only process up to four 'chunks' of information at any one time and confirms, as in the case of the visit above, that plenty of opportunity for practice and review must be offered; and children's attention should be directed through discussion to the essential learning aspects in any situation. Similarly, the child using the clay in the first scenario above did not realize until later that the clay wedges added considerably to the weight or that they could be removed when the clay had dried: these were to become the next 'chunk' in his learning experience.

Nisbet and Shucksmith (1986) argue that insufficient attention has been paid to what essentially they call 'learning how to learn'. They feel that learners are often unaware of the processes in which they have been involved in learning and the decisions and choices they have had to make about what to take on board; yet they feel this is vital in terms of efficiency and productivity in learning. A study into maths teaching and learning by Desforges and Cockburn (1988) would appear to support this view wholeheartedly. They found that the processes were not sufficiently explained and there was no evidence that children could see any relevance in mathematics tasks 'either to the adult world or to their own world outside school' (Desforges and Cockburn, 1988:103). As many of the solutions to problems set for and by the children require mathematical understanding, it is to this area that we now turn. Hughes (1986:169) suggests that:

> In order to solve practical mathematical problems, we need to be capable not only of operating within the formal code, but also of making fluent translations between formal and concrete representations of the same problem.

This problem is evidenced by Duffin (1987) and her adult course participants' attempts at resolving the canoe problem. The task they are set is: 'Two men and two boys want to cross a river. Their canoe will take one man or two boys. How do they all get across?' (Duffin, 1987:88). All agreed that the most understandable solution was effectively a mixture of the mathematical and pictorial. Hughes (1986) believes that teachers must enable children to make such translations understandable and purposive, making children see that there is a point in doing it. In the *First School Survey* (DES, 1982a), HMI suggest that:

> In the schools and classes where play was undervalued the mathematical possibilities of children's play were not developed. (para. 2.75)
>
> Too few schools make good use of opportunities for the development and extension of mathematical understanding which arise in children's play. (para. 4.9)

They go on to say that few children 'have sufficient opportunity for learning how to apply the skills they acquire to the solving of problems' (para. 4.9). The studies by Bennett *et al.* (1984) and Shuard (1984) and the recent research by both Desforges and Cockburn (1988) and Tizard *et al.* (1988) suggest that this is still the case in a majority of schools and that heavy reliance upon commercial schemes prevents teachers from seeing the other opportunities. It is clear that, while paper-and-pencil exercises persist and play is denigrated or neglected, children's opportunities and skills to perform practical problem solving will remain limited or even non-existent. Yet these opportunities exist daily, if only teachers will recognize them and consider how to deal with them. For example, discuss with the children how things might be different in the following situations:

1. Most teachers insist on sitting children down to take the register: most children find it a chore and an inconvenience. What are the needs and possibilities of this situation?
2. Organization of materials. Can the children find everything they want? What are the problems and hindrances to them doing so? How can they be resolved?
3. Misbehaviour, particularly in the playground. What are the causes and how should it be handled?
4. Occasionally, there is a need to get large items into small spaces, e.g. PE apparatus. Why does this need to be done and how best can it be done?
5. Sand and water on the floor constantly create many problems and irritations for adults and children. What are the unique properties which create the difficulties? How might the problems be resolved?
6. Several items within the classroom may well have to be stored so as to be out of the reach of the children – not those for safety purposes of course, but merely the ones for which a convenient lower space is unavailable. What can be done?
7. One group of children constantly dominate the construction toys or the home corner. Why is this? What are their needs? What can be done to satisfy their needs and those of other would-be constructors or role players?
8. The money brought to school for a variety of reasons provides a good resource for considering many different problems such as loss, getting the amount right, indicating who has brought what, and so on.
9. Queues of children. Why do they form? What are the reasons? What might be the solutions?
10. Games and puzzles. How can we ensure that all the pieces are returned to the box? What are the consequences if they are not? What are the reasons for bits going missing and what are the effects?
11. Bullying and gangs are always favourite topics, especially with top infant/first school children. Can they explain the reasons why these groups are formed? Are such groupings necessary? How will everyone else cope with them?

Plate 7. Sometimes, as adults, we forget the delight in the simple!

12. Older children can be set the task of writing a story for younger ones. What attracts younger children to stories? Who and what should the stories be about? How will we find out? How should the story be presented? What can younger children cope with?

The list could go on and on. Sometimes, as adults, we forget the delight in the simple! We disregard the sheer number of events which are commonplace to us but a revelation and excitement to a child. But part of the art of dealing with children is in thinking like a child or, at least, empathizing with children's views. Once adults master this (perhaps through 'playing' with the idea!), they will begin to see many other possibilities and potentialities for problem-solving activities. By allowing children the opportunities in small groups or the whole class to discuss these situations they become personal, purposeful and allow children a platform for verbalizing their thinking. Wells (1985b:39) has confirmed that children need to be able to disengage their thinking from the immediate context of activity and be able to think about real and hypothetical experiences through the medium of words alone. For those children who appear to have some difficulty in this regard, the 'tell me *one* thing you want to know' statement, then 'tell me one thing *more*', usually ensures the development of a list from which to start. Problem solving is also about developing attitudes, particularly the kind of attitude which says 'I don't know why but I want to find out!'

Neither should one be led to believe that only problems of the practical kind require a solution. Children are often presented with moral dilemmas: mummy has said not to go outside the gate but my friend is out there and I want to play with her; the teacher has said I should finish my writing but I really want to play in the new green-coloured water; I can't find my dinner money and the teacher will be cross so should I say that mummy forgot to give it to me? Adults constantly and often unwittingly create these kinds of dilemmas for children and are not always sympathetic when children find their own unique ways around the problem. We should never underestimate children's powers of logical thinking or be surprised when they find novel and occasionally fantastic ways of dealing with situations. Dansky and Silverman (1977:656) remind us that it is within the creative responses of children that we can expect to find the 'fantastic' and that this aids divergent thinking but that children's ideas are not generally 'bizarre', for what they make are associations between events and situations. Ingram (1988:84) confirms that 'although much moral learning takes place implicitly through the life of the school as a community, time needs to be set aside for social and moral education', and that teachers need to 'create a framework of classroom methods and interpersonal relationships which will facilitate such work'.

But do not be led to thinking that as an adult involved with children you can *teach* problem solving (though you can help in the development of strategies) – it must be learned by the learner as every problem has a solution which is unique to that solver (de Bono, 1972:11). Wells (1988:122) concurs, saying that problem solving relies on the 'sense-making strategies that each child has already developed and recognising the individuality of the internal models of the world that each child has already constructed'. Hans (1981:12) feels even more strongly about what play experiences provide for children:

> Play is an experiential mode of confirming or denying the con-
> nections we make with our world and all experience within such a
> mode is confirmed or denied in the playing-out of the experience....
> It can thus occur at many levels and at each level something is

understood and worked through that could not be understood or worked through in any other way.

Making available purposeful, free, exploratory play facilities provides children with active learning through which the many 'preliminaries' of being able to understand and solve problems will be encountered, such as:

1. The opportunity for identifying, recognizing and gaining under-standing of the properties of materials and understanding the nature, function and attributes of familiar and unfamiliar items including the tactile and kinaesthetic.
2. Discovering and distinguishing like and unlike, similar and different elements and characteristics, and matching, sorting and classifying.
3. Discussing within a peer group their explorations and learning with and from other children and contributing adults.
4. Using and describing things in different ways.
5. Representing things in different forms and structures and observing and anticipating transformations and changes.
6. Fitting things together and taking them apart.
7. Arranging and rearranging materials within a given space and experiencing order and sequence.
8. Learning about one's own capabilities, likes and dislikes.
9. Learning to cope with frustration when things do not quite go as planned, e.g. the brick tower falls down, and learning simple cause-and-effect relationships.
10. Learning that time is needed for one to approach and complete a desired task or outcome.

Ample evidence has been presented by such writers as Piaget (1926), Berlyne (1965), Weisler and McCall (1976) and Hutt (1982) to suggest that exploratory play is very likely to be beneficial to subsequent problem-solving activities. These writers identify 'specific exploration' as being that kind of play which looks at what the material is and what it can do, and 'diversive exploration' as essentially leading a child to explore what they can personally do with the material. Children who are more inclined towards diversive exploration (according to Pepler and Rubin, 1982) are also more inclined to trial-and-error learning and its associated opportuni-ties already discussed. Exploration is defined by Sutton-Smith (1986: 143) as exposing oneself to what the object is like and what it can do: play is when one makes it do what one wants it to do.

Directed play, then, can offer the chance to convert this exploratory process into play directed towards a goal which, according to Sylva *et al.* (1977) is a prerequisite to problem solving. This will require that the children are guided into specific observations and reflections on their exploratory play leading to the identification and investigation of a selected 'problem'. This is, of course, best inaugurated by the children, but young children, as has been said, often do not naturally *set* problems, although it may be within their natures to try to resolve them. The second free play bout offers opportunities to children to discover, set and solve their own problems in the light of the previous experiences and leads them to look at further materials or resources which, in their turn, will require exploration before use within the 'restructuring' and 'enrichment' processes (see Chapter 2). 'Practice' and 'revision' will have a firm place within the discursive interactions of children and between children and teacher about how problems are to be resolved and offer possibilities for suggesting alternative solutions. However, Branthwaite and Rogers (1985:i) warn that:

> although older people are cooperative and usually try hard to help, we have to recognize that it is through the mental efforts of the *child* in observing, testing and trying out, that mastery is achieved.

In order to solve problems we need also to have memorized previous events, actions and responses.

Adults involved with children can easily test this out for themselves. Roughly 'match' two groups of children in terms of sex, age and general ability. Allow one group to explore the properties of sticks (or straws) and glue on one or two occasions but give the other group a different and unrelated task. Later, direct both groups to make something from the sticks (or straws) and glue, e.g. a bed for one of the dolls in the doll's house. You may well find that not only do the exploratory play group complete the task with greater facility but that they are also more motivated to achieve something and persevere at the task longer.

The foregoing suggests that it is a simple problem in itself to establish the idea of problem solving with young children. In my experience this is exactly what happens. What it requires, in the early days, is for teachers to be clear what their expectations are of the children and to have suggestions 'up their sleeves' which will both motivate and interest them. They also need to know the capabilities of the materials proffered to children, as sometimes these can be the cause of the problem in themselves, e.g. if children are using Lego to build a tall structure they need some inspired 'direction' as to how best to interlink the bricks. A majority of children under the age of 7 will not discover this for themselves and will get very frustrated without a little direct teaching. Davis (1985) concluded in her study on problem solving that infant school experiences generally increased children's ability to use reflective problem-solving behaviours and further noted that 'disadvantage' through lack of play opportunity at the start of infant school was no longer statistically significant at top infant and lower junior stages.

Interesting school-related problems can be explored with the whole class group, e.g. in one class of 6-year-olds the children constantly complained because the pale coloured wax crayons always produced dark streaks on their pictures. The teacher decided to let the children try to sort out why the problem occurred and what they could do about it. A 'why' question produced answers such as

It's because Amjeet chews them!

Because they get dropped on the floor.

It's because they're all mixed up with the black ones.

In each case possible experiments were tried, such as washing the crayons (which it was eventually agreed was rather laborious), using wider trays on which to store the crayons (giving less opportunity for them to fall on the floor or to become too tightly packed), and putting coloured sticky tape on the end to deter 'chewers'. Eventually, it was decided that the main problem was in mixing the crayons altogether in large tubs. The decision was made that new crayons would be stored in individual colours in individual boxes to see if that made any difference – which it did.

In most of the classroom situations described in this chapter, it has not been a case of leaving the children to set and solve their own problems. The teacher, or other adult, has had a crucial role in:

- monitoring the events;
- advising on actions or materials;
- allowing trial and error to occur (even when to the teacher the result may be obvious);
- providing new materials, information or learning where this was needed (e.g. in the case of the matrix);
- occasionally sustaining interest and motivation;
- listening and responding appropriately to children's explanations;
- expecting the children to 'succeed' (even if only succeeding in finding out that something would not work);
- ensuring the involvement of all the children at whatever level of ability;
- giving feedback, praise and encouragement as necessary;
- providing an appropriately resourced environment in which children can have autonomy; and
- retaining a sense of humour and keeping things in proportion for both themselves and the children;

These are the identified skills of the early childhood educator in relation to problem solving. They seem remarkably similar to descriptions of the role of the effective teacher as described by a number of researchers including Gagne (1970), Evertson and Brophy (1974), Doyle (1983) and

Moyles (1988). Evertson and Brophy (1974:39) even go so far as to suggest that the most effective teachers are those who are geared to 'problem solving techniques for themselves and their pupils'.

There is no doubt that teachers and other adults who provide appropriate challenging play situations for the children both secure and enhance children's learning (Sylva, 1977) and potential learning (Jowett and Sylva, 1986), and enable children to develop higher-order, active thinking strategies. In the *First School Survey* (DES, 1982a), HMI report:

> play was sometimes used by the teacher as a basis for more directed work and with children of all ages their current interests were capitalized upon ... to extend their learning. (para. 3.11)

In schools where this happened, the majority of children achieved 'better levels of performance across a wide range of their work' (ibid., para. 3.11). Problem-solving situations also require the child to concentrate which is important in terms of remembering, which in turn allows alternative strategies to be built up. As Brierley (1987:92) suggests: 'a child remembers only those things to which he pays keen attention. None of the things he ignores appears to leave a memory trace in the brain.' Obviously, the more memorable we can make all learning the better. Vygotsky's words of wisdom are well worth mentioning here, for he says that 'The child moves forward essentially through play activity', and he suggests that play can 'be termed a leading activity which determines the child's development' (Vygotsky, 1932:552).

For centuries games such as chess have provided players with challenges. Some writers believe that gaming is at the heart of play. Strictly, gaming is play in the context of rules (Piaget, 1951) and is the main type of play which persists in adulthood. But problems can also be presented to children in terms of games. Hughes (1986) believes strongly that in mathematics games are the answer to problems of purpose and representation. Strategy and adventure games abound in the computer world and I have known children as young as 7 years of age spend several hours trying to solve the problem of the missing children in *Granny's Garden*. At present, computer and video games sometimes deny children one major opportunity – that of playing *with* and negotiating with other children – which has been identified as a major component in successful problem-setting and -solving. In fact, Sutton-Smith (1986:63) describes video games as the ultimate in solitary play, which rather than supporting cooperation and competition between individuals, the game strategy becomes one of an individual attempting to beat the machine. Simon (1985) believes that computers used imaginatively will become a tool that can enrich the environment of all children, particularly in relation to their play.

Successful problem solving with young children may not happen overnight. The adults involved need time to adjust their methods and the children will need to be fed with ideas through a variety of activities and discussions. The Cockcroft Report (DES, 1982b) suggested that 'The ability to solve problems is at the heart of maths.' I would contend that the word maths could be substituted by language, science, physical education, dance, drama, technology, art and, of course, play – and the same thing would apply. Problem solving links the intellectual with the practical: it links basic skills with higher-order ones; it links teaching with learning; it links direction with choice – essentially, it links play with 'work'. Because of young children's abilities to interchange between reality and fantasy, they are frequently capable of producing very unconventional but very creative solutions to problems. They are also capable of creativity in another sense, that of being artistically creative, on which the next chapter will now focus.

5

Play and Creativity

Scenarios

1. The full-length mirror in the home corner has become the focus of attention of a 4-year-old. She moves her head from side to side, then moves herself, turns around, sits down, stands up and then tries to turn herself upside-down, peering into the mirror at all times. She then moves close to the mirror and enquires of the image, 'How are you today?' The 'image' smiles, then giggles and then attempts to hold hands. The child then moves away from the mirror, selects a number of hats from the dressing-up rack, and, sitting in front of the mirror once more, dons hat after hat, talking to herself all the time, until she is satisfied with one in particular. The others are discarded to the floor and another 3 minutes or so is spent in talking to the mirror image, resplendent in hat, about the weather, taking the children to school, going to a wedding and, finally, dismissing herself with a wave. Still wearing the preferred hat, the child then moves over to a table where crayons and paper are available and draws a family of people all wearing different hats and smiling broadly!

2. A 5-year-old is just finishing a painting of some chicks, recently hatched in the classroom, which the teacher has suggested they may choose to paint. From the form of her figures she obviously has a good sense of shape, balance, proportion and she has used colour appropriately. The child stands back a little, looks slightly puzzled, puts her brush back carefully in the pot and walks over to have a further look at the chicks. She kneels on the floor, peers intently into the tray in which the chicks are housed for a minute or two, and then walks back to the painting table. Very deliberately she takes up a rather thick brush full of blue paint and moves it across the paper, seemingly intending to add an eye to one of her chicks. In so doing, however, the blue paint dribbles on to the edge of the paper. She moves the brush backwards and forwards a little around the edge of the paper creating more dribbles in which she obviously gains both interest and pleasure. The chicks are forgotten as brush after brush of

Plate 8. The young child painting chicks.

different coloured paints is dribbled carefully and methodically around the edge of the paper making a very effective patterned border to the picture. In what looks like a final flourish with the sixth or seventh colour the child has just lifted the brush out of the pot when an adult comes across: 'Oh dear, don't spoil your lovely picture of the chicks! Here, let me put your name on it and we'll put it in the drying rack before it gets spoilt.'

For the purposes of a suitable presentation, there has been an implicit suggestion that language, problem solving and creativity are not particularly related. This is, of course, not the case, and this chapter will attempt to expand on features of the previous two chapters as well as add new thoughts on the issues. However, creativity is as difficult a term to define as play itself. According to Marzollo and Lloyd (1972:162): 'Creativity is basically an attitude, one that comes easily to young children, but must be sustained and strengthened lest it be sacrificed in our too logical world.' The first scenario above adds some support to this view and will be discussed in greater detail later. Claxton (1984:124) suggests that ' ''creativity'' is not a trait but a process that may occur in a certain *state*, and that state is relaxed but alert receptivity'.

The correlation between creativity and problem solving has already been made in terms of the child as divergent and logical thinker. Guilford (1957:112) contends that 'It is in divergent thinking that we find the most obvious indications of creativity.' The links exist in many ways and are

---, ..terrelated but there are some differences. Problem solving, as we have seen in the previous chapter, is basically goal-oriented, attempting to find alternatives or solutions – be they concrete or abstract in nature – and is highly cognitively oriented. Creativity lies similarly within the cognitive domain but also exerts a stronger influence on the affective domain and is about personal expression and interpretation of emotions, thoughts and ideas: it is a process which outweighs any product particularly, as we shall see, for the young child. According to Brierley (1987:67): 'creativity is the capacity to respond emotionally and intellectually to sensory experiences'. It is also closely related to being 'artistic' in the broadest sense of the word. This may be considered to be rather an arbitrary definition but one that is vital in attempting to look at another aspect of children's play and learning in that creativity has strong ties with aesthetics education.

If we accept that being able to express oneself effectively is a 'good' outcome of education then nowhere is this more likely to happen for young children than in creative activities associated with play. The child as 'creator' appears in a majority of play contexts, two of which have already been cited above. Children constantly create and recreate ideas and images which enable them to represent and come to terms with themselves and their views of reality. These can be captured in children's talk, drawing and painting, craft, design, music, dance, drama and, of course, play. We can all be creative within our heads in the way we interpret what we receive. We can similarly show creativity by the way in which we are able to express ourselves in a variety of media be it words, paint, clay or whatever. The expressive activities of 4-year-olds will at first represent that which has impressed a child in real-life situations, but within a year or two children will quickly become more imaginative and creative as their ability to symbolize increases. Meek asserts that creativity and imagination are rooted in all young children's play and, therefore, part of every child's repertoire, rather than that of a gifted few. She feels strongly that they constitute the basis of the real business of education (Meek, 1985:41).

Creativity, then, is inextricably linked with the arts, language and the development of representation and symbolism. Symbolic play is also about order and assists in the development of planning skills. It eventually leads to the beginning of rule-based play and games (Piaget, 1950). The importance of this is stressed by Currie and Foster (1975:8):

Children try and symbolize the real, physical world through their play and through art. In both of these outlets, past experiences are repeated and relived. In this way, we can relate our external world of reality to our internal one of past experiences and knowledge, mental organisation and interpretive power. We can link new experiences to old ones and so our minds absorb new information and expand.

The scenarios, which show this effectively in practical terms within the classroom situation, reflect the main reason for incorporating a whole chapter on creative expression in an endeavour to emphasize its very important nature and the need for adults to consider creativity and all its associations in greater depth.

The word 'creative' is used in school quite widely and rather as blanket terminology. 'Creative writing' and 'creative dance' are in general use but are capable of such wide interpretation that they have little real meaning. Creative writing, for example, embraces a multiplicity of writing styles which cover purely functional writing about going to grandma's for tea, through transactional writing about doing a simple experiment, to poetic writing about the big, black spider Joanne found on the way to school! Creative dance similarly includes radio programmes which heavily direct young children's movement, through dancing to music and country and folk dancing to name but a few. It is more helpful to everyone if we can be a little more specific about what we mean by being creative.

However, we all need something or some experience in which to be creative and express our creativity just as we all need to play. Some people put their efforts to practical use (e.g. internal decor, flower arranging, planning gardens, cordon bleu cookery, making clothes), whereas others, for example, draw, write poetry or paint as an outlet. Many adults sit lengths of time literally daydreaming about holidays, friendships, winning the pools, retirement, and so on which, in effect, is equivalent to a child fantasizing. In the second scenario above, paint was the child's medium for expression, whereas, in the first, it was imagination and fantasizing, albeit eventually leading to commitment of the experience to paper.

It could be said that play naturally leads to creativity because children are required at all levels of play to use skills and processes which provide opportunities to be creative. Additional to the problem solving already explored and the skills of coordination and manipulation vital to expressing oneself physically or through other media, a search of the literature in this area indicates that creativity is related to children's development and understanding of

- representation
- spatial relations
- shape, form and line
- balance
- colour
- pattern
- texture
- discrimination
- perception
- interpretation
- kinaesthetic awareness
- sensory pleasure
- communication
- choice
- shared and personal meanings
- concrete and abstract thought
- flexibility
- sensitivity
- planning abilities
- purpose

- experimentation   • sense of audience
- visual awareness

Most vitally is the interrelationship with language: the close links with pretend play, literature and poetry have already been discussed in Chapter 3, as has the need for a wealth of opportunities for children to talk and explain. According to Almy (1977:207–8), free exploration of materials must lead teachers to enquire what children have found out, thus ensuring that children are activated to use language. This is unlikely to be a problem when children have had wide experiences of expressing themselves in other ways first. Support is also given to this notion by Curtis (1986:62), who states that an adequate development of language is dependent upon the amount of practice children have in speaking about their experiences.

However, it must be remembered that art in itself is a form of communication without words, as anyone who has ever seen a mime artist or a completely breathtaking painting will confirm. Children and adults who, for whatever reason, have difficulty in communicating through language can often express themselves vividly in other media and gain comfort and self-esteem in being able to do so. Those who feel they cannot paint often have beautifully expressive bodily movement capabilities, those who are clumsy in gross motor activities can sometimes find music and rhythm a source of inspiration or acting the role of someone else in drama or through puppetry can inspire non-verbal and verbal communication in others.

So in art forms, as in different forms of play, there lies a wealth of creative opportunity for children and adults both for expressing their own thinking and for appreciating the artistry of others. Adults do not always recognize children's artistic endeavours, as with the child in the second scenario above, for many adults get locked into ideas of appropriate representation, i.e. the notion that a picture should be photographic and present graphically exact likenesses of what they represent. We all receive 'art' as well as create it ourselves, and most of us know what we like because of our personalities, experiences, knowledge and our own capabilities or otherwise to express ourselves in forms communicable to others. Children present the world as they see it and as they are capable of representing it at a particular time in their development: beauty is there if we are prepared to behold it, for one of the difficulties of art is that it is riddled with values, all of which we have acquired through our own cultures and upbringing. De Bono (1972:8) suggests that this is not always such a good thing from an artistic standpoint:

> From time to time every creative person wishes he had the outlook of a child so that he could find his own perceptions and escape from the ones that have been imposed on him.

The perceptions children have of life are, as we have already seen, bound up very closely within a world where fantasy and reality constantly go hand-in-hand. Research has shown that the children who indulge freely in good quality fantasy and pretend play, the children who are considered to be 'high fantasizers' and spend a good deal of time in imaginative thinking (Singer and Singer, 1977; Pulaski, 1981; Riess 1981), have greater tendencies towards being creative with materials and situations. Such studies have also found that these creative, internal thinkers have better concentration, are less aggressive generally, can tell more creative stories with greater originality and more complex characters and situations, and are more inclined to enjoy what they do than children who are 'low fantasizers'. Studies such as those cited led Freyberg (1981) to feel that creative play training for children who were 'low fantasizers' would increase their general creativity. She used pipe-cleaner people, playdough, bricks and small toys to act out make-believe adventures and then encouraged the children to tell stories likewise. After eight sessions, using the Singers' test of imaginative play predisposition, Freyberg found that direct teaching had not only increased children's ability to fantasize but had increased attention spans, verbal communication and enjoyment.

Before they can understand, represent and recreate shape, colour, form, balance, structure, texture, and so on, children must play with materials and resources which provide a means towards developing such understandings, knowledge, concepts and skills. They must also explore their environment and their experiences in detail rather than cursorily, as is usually the case with the young child who actually finds it difficult to take in 'whole' or complete images and tends to dwell on only one or two facets of particular interest (Sloboda, 1985). The child of 6, whose drawing of a horse is shown in Fig. 5.1, highlights everything that can be said about a young child being able to create and represent from her own experiences. The drawing is exceptional for a child of her age and shows a simplicity of line and form which has many similarities with cave paintings. Her relationship and understanding of this animal was also exceptional: she spent every available moment with the animal, grooming it, riding it, exploring it in all senses and with all her senses.

The image then produced is very much her own, based on a very immediate and meaningful reality. Pulaski insists that children must have this kind of content in order to create: 'They cannot', she says, 'produce a meaningful imitation of say, a carnival, unless they know what a carnival is' (Pulaski, 1981:18). I would add that the child also needs to know not only what it looks like but also its smells, sounds, sensations, peculiarities and her feelings about it, which are all in evidence from Kate's picture of her horse. Most children given this level of saturation would produce quality drawings. Goodnow (1977:10) could be writing of this child's drawing when she says 'Most of them have charm, novelty, simplicity,

Fig. 5.1. A child's drawing of her own horse.

playfulness and a fresh approach that is a source of pure pleasure.' Not all children, however, will be fortunate enough to have this child's experience in their daily lives. Some can be given that experience, as were the children whose drawings are shown as Figs 5.2 and 5.3 who, keenly interested in birds, were taken on a visit to a bird sanctuary and produced these pictures as a result. Equally though, some children will have had little opportunity outside school to express themselves in a wide variety of media and will need many experiences of sand, water, clay, paint, crayons, felt pens, junk materials, textiles and fabrics, cottons and threads, opportunities for expressive movement, the chance to make and hear music or write and hear poetry and stories.

It is clear that the time required for a full exploration of a wide variety of materials and resources will differ from child to child and there should be no expectation of 'product' by the adult during this period. End-products will, however, inevitably be created and those intent on displaying the classroom to good effect will no doubt be relieved! It needs to be remembered at this time that the classroom itself should stimulate and

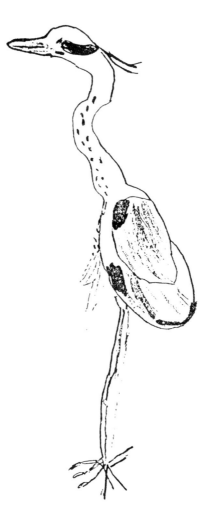

Fig. 5.2. A child's drawing from deep personal interest and experience.

inspire exploration and the adults can create displays and interesting corners of particular materials for children to explore. It should be emphasized, however, that this does not mean getting children to fill in outlines drawn by the adults. HMI, in the *First School Survey* (DES, 1982a, para. 2.144), warn that the creative and educational value of some of the work was 'very slight when, for example children were using crayons or tissue paper to fill in outlines drawn by the teacher or were drawing around templates'.

Adults need to value what the children themselves, through their own creative expression, eventually produce: they must not produce it for them. Bruce (1987:58) feels as strongly as I do about this:

Fig. 5.3. A further child's drawing from deep personal interest and experience.

> Being able to reproduce someone else's idea of a cat by means of a stencil is low-level work. Helping children to use what they can do – draw circles and lines – tells them that they can draw their own cat, unique, special, imaginative. This is a higher level skill in the child and needs careful encouragement from adults.

The role of the teacher must be in observing, initiating, participating, encouraging, maintaining and extending children's art experiences. Let us return for a while to the second scenario at the start of this chapter which raises a number of issues both philosophical and practical in relation to children, creativity, art and play.

The child's delight in her own aesthetically pleasing discovery was apparent from a moment's glance. The fact that she had almost tired of the observational aspect of her painting of the chicks is another and raises the whole question of attentional span. The practical issue of having a wide variety of different coloured paints for the task in hand is also interesting. The chicks downy feathers were various shades of yellow moving through into white and they had rather orange feet; they were housed in a pale yellow tray containing sawdust and, apart from their slightly darker eyes, the whole scene was one of pastel colours within a fairly limited spectrum. Yet the children had been provided with non-spill pots of black, red, blue, yellow, green, brown and purple paint. There was no white and no suggestion within the provision of any kind of mixing tray or water. So what, you might be heard to say, children can imagine things any colour they want them to be – that is what being creative is all about – but this leads us to question the purpose of the activity and the opportunities provided within it to be creative. In the early stages the child has obviously taken seriously the idea of painting the chicks and had used the yellow paint to create the forms she interpreted from what she saw. She even went to check on the eye colouring and perhaps position, but eventually, possibly through waning concentration or the effects of an overly large brush with which to paint a tiny eye or the variety of colours, she was drawn away from her previous creation and diverted to another. There are certain features of this that are worthy of further consideration:

1. Having set an observational task rather than a total free painting situation the providing adults needed to consider the appropriateness of the materials. The child could have been equally creative with her picture and perhaps more so if a limited range of colours appropriate to the set task had been available.
2. Pre-teaching and experimentation of the techniques of mixing paints to get a desired effect may have resulted in greater exploration by the child of the colour range possible from orange, through yellow into white.
3. Provision of water and a mixing tray, even without preliminary exposition of techniques, could well have meant that the child would experiment herself with pastel shades and explore the effects.
4. Different sized brushes are very vital for different purposes, even for 5-year-olds.
5. The consistency of the paint may have needed to be considered more fully.
6. Free painting opportunities allow different kinds of creativity from directed forms.
7. Pre-planning of the experiences adults wish children to have is essential if learning within the school context is to be appropriately tailored to children's development and needs.
8. How the teacher approaches the whole question of creativity in terms of artistic expression is very significant if children's future explorations are to be fruitful and enjoyable.

The important feature of this is that creative activity of any kind does not just happen. Being creative is also about planning what you want to happen. Children do this intuitively to a certain extent, but intuition is based on experience. A wealth of past experiences with paper and paints will suggest to a child where to begin – we all know the child who, unfamiliar with planning and organizing the creation of a large figure, ends up with painting a tall person with very short legs in order to complete the person within the confines of the paper! This is, of course, related to the child's stage of development, but sometimes these supposed stages of development are underestimated. For example, I have taught children aged under 6 years that the sky meets the land for the purposes of pictures and I have introduced them to wash techniques that enable them to meet land and sky successfully without a heavier paint preventing this understanding. No doubt one could argue that the medium provides the message in this case and that the children are not, in fact, learning that the land meets the sky but that they can do this with the medium. However, when one considers that such art techniques as were introduced were also used in the context of several weeks of observing the land and sky from different places and angles, for different purposes, it could also equally be that the children had gained understanding earlier than when such things are left to chance.

There is no doubt that we have to encourage creativity and artistic expression through providing children with the appropriate techniques and materials with which to explore the potential of a situation or event. Other teachers of my acquaintance have also found that providing children with a limited range of colours of paint, crayon and felt tip and/or different shades of paint (e.g. pastel shades), has led to children expressing themselves in quite different ways from when presented with the usual range of primary colours plus green, brown and purple. Similarly with dance – opportunities to create and use different spaces (outside on tarmac or grass, inside in the classroom or hall) create different atmospheres in which physical expressions may take place, as similarly do different stimuli. Recreating the movements of autumn trees produces very different movement forms and expression than recreating anger, happiness or darkness. The same is true of musical expressions – making music to accompany songs presents children with very different challenges from creating music to accompany a walk through a haunted house or across a snowy field. Setting up a home corner as Red Riding Hood's grandma's cottage is a form of dramatic role play associated with re-representation of established images: true imaginative role play allows children to present and interpret images they themselves have created through their own perceptions of fantasy and reality. 'Dramatic play', says Needles (1980:189) is 'a crucial ingredient in the consolidation of *thinking* skills.'

It is sometimes forgotten that children are highly creative using a variety of constructional toys. They build mini-worlds in which they play out pretend and fantasy situations. Seven-year-olds of my acquaintance happened one day, on moving classrooms, to rediscover a huge box of wooden building bricks of various shapes and sizes. In the next 2 hours, and to the amazement of the teacher who thought that they had 'grown out' of such toys, they created a whole settlement stretching at least 3 metres across the carpet. It had every conceivable facility for births, marriages and deaths, war and peace, manufacture and the general paraphernalia of everyday living, as well as a few creative touches like a cave for the local dragon and a platform on which alien spacecraft could land! The children were able not only to model this 'world' but to change it at will, draw it, measure it, write about its events, share its meanings with others as well as enjoy it personally, think about the life it represented chronologically and temporally and create for it with other bits and pieces when needs were discovered. These kinds of open-ended play materials have been found by several researchers to be highly conducive to creative play; for example, Pepler (1982) and Rubin and Howe (1985) report that more abstract toys and materials encourages children's creative play and that more highly structured materials lead to greater creative expression.

Creativity and the current play theory

These previous examples, in a whole variety of ways, enable us to see where the current models of play and learning closely interact in relation to children's creativity. Any exploration of creative media and experience highlights the processes; directed activities then focus the children's attention on the learning of different techniques which, in turn, frees them to play and recreate with increased knowledge, skills and understanding. According to Jeanrenaud and Bishop (1980:81):

> Moderate directiveness ... is most likely to lead to creativity. Although the children's approach and exploration are experienced as spontaneous, they actually follow a predetermined path leading to the discovery of appropriate responses.

When children have had many opportunities and experiences for using their imaginations and creating different effects and emotions through their art activities, they can be guided into more challenges through design-related art. One group of 7-year-olds were asked at this stage to make a raincoat for a rag doll. They first of all wanted to make the doll look pretty but then got more deeply into the functional nature of a mackintosh. They explored, experimented with and tested a variety of materials in order to find one which proved water-repellent. From this they designed a raincoat which would cover the doll from its head down to its ankles because, of course, rag dolls get soggy when they are wet! They drew around the doll to form a kind of net in order that they would get the right size – they forgot, however, that in gluing the parts together the size would be reduced. With trial and error and an analysis of what had gone well the first time, they then made another totally successful mackintosh. Without prompting, at a later session, they also made an umbrella and some wellingtons. This ability to select materials and understand which ones will give the desired result is seen by Pluckrose (1984) to be most significant in children establishing aesthetic principles.

Science and technology can easily intermingle with art for young children but what must be emphasized is that the processes of design, choice, shared meanings, interpretation and all the items previously listed, were far more important to both children and directing adult than what transpired eventually to be a successful garment. This is, as has been asserted before, where problem solving and creativity meet but equally diverge. Child (1985:57) believes that creative thinking depends upon context, asking 'How do we correlate the inventive activities and output of a famous scientist, a famous artist and a small child?'

Children are naturally makers of marks; they scribble from a very early age and, as symbolic thinking develops, the marks made change their significance and powers of representation. Young children can clearly be seen apparently developing a model of a house in clay which, moments later, has changed into a structure more resembling a monster. Seconds later it has become an amorphous mass on the table. How can adults evaluate what has been learned aesthetically or cognitively? Only later, when the children are able, following their own explorations, to satisfy themselves with some particular form and explain it to others can adults begin to assess cognitive processes. Towards the middle of the 4- to 8-year-old period, children want peers and adults to understand their pictures and models but, before then, according to Pluckrose (1984:256), 'imagination overrides the restriction imposed by space, time or by the materials that are available. He constructs because he has to.' Just as I contend, the child has to play.

'To be creative you have to dare to be different' (Claxton, 1984:228). Being creative requires time and imagination, both of which most children have available to them. More importantly, being creative requires self-trust, some knowledge, receptivity, a sense of nonsense and the ability to play, all of which are well within the realms of childhood and many of which need to be engendered with greater vigour in the context of school and education.

PART THREE

6

Play, Curriculum and Organization

✦

Scenarios

1. A group of five 6-year-olds is gathered around a table fingerprinting with blue and yellow paints. The activity is part of a topic on colour. They are variously representing different shapes of their choosing – a person, flowers, a tree, a fish – and one child is making abstract patterns. This child presses a yellow fingerprint carefully over a blue one, looks hard at it, and then repeats the action. He turns to his neighbour, points at what has happened and says 'Look, I've made it go green!' The second child tries it out with a similar result. They both call excitedly to the teacher to come and look. She comes over and says 'Tell me what's been happening.' The child describes in some detail how he placed yellow over blue and made green and then how he repeated it to show his friend. The teacher asks: 'Do you think you could make any other colours?' The child responds 'I think so.' This time he puts yellow paint on his paper and adds a blue print: 'Look, I've made a green again but its darker!' The teacher says 'So you have. I wonder if you can make any more shades of green?' The child painting the tree begins to streak her fingers gently across the yellow and blue blobs and 'magically' they turn to green. She begins to talk animatedly about her discovery. The teacher asks what they would like to do with or about their discovery. One child suggests they get some brushes and 'little trays' and mix some blue and yellow in different ways. The children fetch trays and brushes while the teacher organizes more paper. She quietly adds yellow and blue paper to the white the children already have. The children continue to experiment discussing with each other what they are doing and the shades of colour they are making, and the activity continues for over an hour. At the end of the session the children report back with the results of their experiments.

2. The teacher has gathered the whole class of 27 five-year-olds around her to show them an experiment on which materials keep things warm. It is part of a topic on 'Hot and Cold' which is currently underway. She has four empty baked-bean tins covered with fur fabric, tin foil, newspaper and cotton material, respectively. She tells the children they are going to test which one keeps the water hot for the rest of the afternoon and that they will periodically gather round to test which is remaining warm. The children watch as she pours hot water from the kettle into the tins and puts a further circle of material over the top. Two children are then invited to feel the outside of the tins. The teacher asks: 'Which one is the warmest at the moment?' One child looks blank, the other says 'This one', which is the one she is holding at the time. The teacher asks: 'Can anyone think why this one is the warmest?' A lot of shaking of heads and murmuring ensues. The teacher then asks: 'Which one do you think will still be warm at the end of the afternoon?' A number of individual children proffer suggestions, all different. She asks one child who has opted for the foil-covered tin to say why she thinks that one. The child answers 'Because its shiny.' At this point several children are getting fidgety and the teacher sends them off in groups to do their maths books, hot and cold printing and copy writing. Towards the end of the afternoon the children tidy away and return to a discussion about the experiment. The teacher reiterates what happened earlier in the afternoon and asks the children if they can think which tin will now be the hottest. A variety of guesses is made though no children can give a reasoned answer for their choice. 'Well, I think its cool enough now that we can ask someone to put their finger in and test it for us' says the teacher. Several children volunteer, Amdeep is chosen and duly pushes his finger into each tin consecutively.

Teacher: Which one feels the hottest?
Amdeep: I don't know.
Teacher: Come on now, try again.

Amdeep tries again but looks more and more puzzled. 'I think we must give someone else a try' says the teacher. Robert is chosen. He, too, looks very puzzled and cannot answer. The teacher then suggests that she does it herself and declares the fur-fabric covered tin the 'winner':

Teacher: What kind of material will keep us warmest in the winter then?
Child: Pink, furry stuff!

There is no doubt that adults should not underestimate their influence on children and children's play. A major potential difficulty as well as potential joy is that children want so much to please the adults with whom they come into regular contact and to do what they appear to want. This is a tremendous responsibility for those within whose hands the education of the youngest children rests, for it means that manipulation of young minds and actions is relatively easy and we must be very clear what our intentions are if we are not to abuse this quite phenomenal power. Just how far children will go to 'please the teacher' in the school context has been shown by King (1978), Bennett *et al.* (1984) and Desforges and Cockburn (1988). Despite an underlying premise in this book, and in most others to do with early education, that children must see a purpose and be actively involved in what they are doing, this has frequently been shown in such studies as those cited above, to be singularly not the case.

The complementary nature of teaching and learning

Isolating features of classroom life is not only dangerous but often gives a distorted picture. The day is so complex and diverse that to adopt any one part of it for discussion may be doing all participants an injustice. However, the two scenarios above were chosen because they show very different responses and strategies on the part of the teachers concerned and there are many issues which both present to all early childhood educators. The main issue, however, must be in looking at the complementary nature of teaching and learning. There is no single teaching style or, indeed, one learning style which can be applied across all situations and all teachers and children. All of us use different tactics dependent upon our philosophies and views of education and learning and these, in turn, are influenced by personality, mood, the educational environment, levels of support, facilities and resources – the list is endless. Much has been written in Britain since the early 1970s on the styles of teaching and their effects on children's progress (Bennett, 1976; Galton *et al.*, 1980; Nash, 1984) and the market is swamped with American literature on these issues (e.g. Mohan and Hull, 1972; Millman, 1981; Combs, 1982). Despite this, nobody is yet absolutely clear where the correlations lie, due undoubtedly to the very complex nature of primary teaching. However, documents such as those produced by HMI (e.g. DES, 1985a, 1987a) do highlight certain features of good practice which have been identified in a variety of schools and these emphasize that the quality of teaching and learning is dependent upon a number of factors related to:

- the active involvement of children (brain activity as much as physical activity) in their learning;
- the relevance and purpose of what children are expected to do and the close relationship it has with their own lives;
- the teacher's implicit organization for learning and provision of a broad, balanced and differentiated curriculum;
- classroom management situations which ensure children have independence in their learning and expectations of self-discipline rather than it being imposed;

- high expectations of children and an opportunity to work and play in practical problem-solving situations; and
- the development of attitudes which foster learning and encourage cooperation, concentration and willingness.

Play in the curriculum

It is clear that many of these factors operate within what might be called a play curriculum but this ignores a major feature of play, i.e. play is a process which provides a mode for learning and results in play behaviours. These in themselves do not provide a curriculum but an invaluable means for initiating, promoting and sustaining learning within a curriculum framework (a basis for which is explored a little later). Encouraging play as a learning medium and sustaining motivation and interest through play are strategies equal to direct instruction. Just as teachers see complete relevance in setting children written objectives (e.g. the completion of a page of sums or writing a story about what they did over the weekend), they must be prepared to see equal (if not greater) value in setting children play objectives, examples of which have been explored in previous chapters. Several schools have explored the idea of a 'play policy' and a post-holder responsible for 'play' in the school, and these are positive moves in attempting to promote the recognition of the role of play. However, because play is a process rather than a subject, it is really within subjects that one should look to play as a means of teaching and learning rather than as a separate entity. Because of the relevance and motivation of play to children, play must pervade how teachers present potential learning activities, not sit as an uncomfortable and somewhat suspect activity in itself.

Most teachers do say that they feel play is valuable and has a place in the classroom, yet most also by their attitudes indicate implicitly that it does not have a prime place but is rather secondary to the activities which they themselves direct and supervise. Particularly in infant schools, however, there is no evidence at all that this directive teaching actually promotes children's real learning (see Bennett *et al.*, 1984; Desforges and Cockburn, 1988; Tizard *et al.*, 1988), for it rarely starts from where the children are ready to begin. Teachers are teaching from the level and standpoint they think the children *should* be at rather than from a real understanding of where the children actually are. This appears to stem from the view of teacher as instructor who knows what needs to be taught and proceeds to teach it, a position perhaps exemplified in the second scenario above. The teacher in the paint-mixing scenario was much more inclined to the notion that children should, as far as possible, be allowed to explore the materials and activities themselves, that they will then require direction to further their learning and, finally, that another exploratory play session will help to develop their experience further.

Early childhood education has come a long way, however, particularly through nursery practices which have shown clearly that children do, indeed, develop cognitively and affectively from play within a well-organized environment (Jowett and Sylva, 1986). How sad, then, that Tizard and her colleagues still report in 1988 that in 33 London schools researched, children in top infant classes spend less than *one percent* of their day in 'free' play activities (Tizard *et al.*, 1988:49). Yet while classes of 30 or more children to 1 adult persist as the norm, this amounts to very little adult time per child, or even group of children. In itself, however, this statement must make teachers consider carefully what their role is in the classroom. If the role is viewed as one of instructor, teachers must 'instruct' or teach something directly to everyone every day – a very hard task for one person. If, however, the teacher's role is one of initiator and enabler of learning and as provider of the framework within which children can explore, play, plan and take responsibility for their own learning, this puts a very different complexion on things. More importantly, this approach surely frees teachers to spend more time with the children in exploring learning and understanding? It becomes more a matter of the teacher as effective organizer of the prospective learning situation within which she or he then acknowledges, affirms and supports the children's opportunities to learn in their own way, at their own level and from their own past experiences.

Lest all this begins to sound idealistic, there is now clearly a need to suggest a framework in which play and learning can take place to everyone's advantage.

An early childhood curriculum

curriculum is by definition about the transmission of values. (Winkley, 1987:193)

It is also about intentions, content, actions and outcomes. But more importantly it is about, in this case, young children and the variety and richness they bring with them as a starting point. HMI have been keen to acknowledge in a whole range of reports that the primary curriculum operated from a topic-based, experiential and integrated approach has a great deal to commend it and all reports have favoured this stance at the expense of a 'basic skills' approach. Richards (1987:168) says of a national curriculum:

Far from devaluing the work of class teachers ... [it] would increase their standing by fully recognizing the formidable range and levels of demand now being made upon them and by involving them, not just in the planning of the work of their own classes, but in the establishment of a school-wide curricular framework.

The reality of the situation now is indeed one of a directed National Curriculum and the urge within all of us is to try to defend what we already do: anything new at this time of great flux in education, is a pressure we can do without! But as Richards above suggests, teachers are in no way being deprived of the use of their professional skills. What is being suggested is that, in having intentions and content set within a framework which we all understand and value, we are actually 'freed' to do a better job as principal agents of quality education; we still put the curriculum into action. What of the arguments regarding the lack of considerations of the developing child within a national structure? If we look objectively at the aims of the National Curriculum reiterated below, there does not appear to be any real conflict between a child development approach to teaching and learning and the planned curriculum. It is still possible to work within Bruner's (1971) approach of starting where the child is – *if* we are prepared as teachers to look beyond the rather heavy overtones of the document to what we know and believe is right for the children. The framework is essentially one of developmental issues, knowledge and values and one is led to question: 'Is this not what adults have been attempting to transmit to children all along?'

Another point worthy of mention here, although the National Curriculum encompasses children from 5 years of age upwards, there are now many 4-year-olds in reception classes throughout the country who are to all intents and purposes being deemed mainstream children and to whom the National Curriculum will, therefore, apply. The *Curriculum from 5 to 16* document (DES, 1981), the aims of which have been reiterated in the National Curriculum paper (DES, 1987b), states clearly that it is the purpose of schools to help children to:

1. Develop lively, enquiring minds and have the ability to question and argue rationally and to apply themselves to tasks.
2. Acquire knowledge and skills relevant to adult life and employment in a fast changing world.
3. Use language and numbers effectively.
4. Instil respect for religious and moral values, and tolerance of other races, religions and ways of life.
5. Help pupils to understand the world in which they live and the interdependence of individuals, groups and nations.
6. Appreciate human achievements and aspirations.

However, as stated by the Schools Council (1983:16): 'Aims such as these may seem too broad and vague to be of any great practical help to practising teachers.' They are, but therein also lies their strength, for how it is achieved is then up to schools and teachers. The further suggestion is that these aims should be manifest in a curriculum whose content should include nine 'subject' areas: maths, language, science, technology, geography, history, art and design, PE, drama and music. Within these the curriculum should be broad, balanced, relevant, have continuity and take account of differing needs. The National Curriculum document (DES, 1987b) itself stresses that, for primary education, these subject areas need to be considered in a more integrated framework. My own feeling is that I would like to make an addition to (3) above to suggest that children should be able to use effectively *all* their acquired learning in the many other curriculum areas and not just those related to language and numbers. However, once again, this is a pedanticism against the terminology which need not apply if one adopts the view that was taken in Chapter 3 that language in itself is all pervasive of humanities, science, problem solving, and so on.

The fact is that the curriculum for a long time has been viewed very much more narrowly within many schools than the stated aims above, with a major concentration being put on the development of knowledge and practice skills at the expense of other areas. Similarly, maths (mostly numbers) and language (mostly reading and writing), particularly in infant schools, have been major constituents of the curriculum, again at the expense of other important areas, hence the earlier chapters in this book on problem solving and creativity, two issues which have had little prominence so far in many schools' curricula but which require far more attention if we are to consider the whole child developmentally.

What adults must do is to calculate how much time is spent within the classroom, usually in infant and first schools within a topic framework, on the various elements of the curriculum. What is insufficiently covered in one topic can be compensated for in another and, therefore, it is important when planning topics or areas of interest with the children that balance is taken into account, and where one topic lends itself more specifically to an arts-based emphasis the next one might have a science emphasis.

If we were to take a topic-based, integrated week and disintegrate it for a while, what would we find? Working with early years student teachers, I see a great deal of planning for a broad, balanced, relevant and progressive curriculum and, while accepting that teaching practice is not altogether typical of on-going, year-in, year-out teaching, it tends to reflect not only 'good' practice but also the regime of the class teacher whom the student replaces. A quick survey of the plans of 12 students in a variety of infant schools and departments revealed that in an ordinary 5-hour day, students planned for approximately:

- 90 minutes of language activities, including story times, finger plays and oral discussion sessions (frequently about maths, science, art and humanities);
- 90 minutes of maths activities, often associated with related science

work and the setting and solving of problems through free and directed play;

- about 60 minutes of art activities. This appears disproportionate in terms of National Curriculum requirements but, on closer inspection, much of the art work was related to shape (maths), observation drawings (science), structures or model making (technology) and quite often related to the world around them (humanities). Perhaps 15 minutes might be classed as 'pure' art, leaving 45 minutes of the remaining time to science, technology and humanities;
- at least 20 minutes each day was usually given to music, PE, dance or drama;
- another 20 minutes for preparing children to go to lunch, out to play, into assembly; and
- a further 20 minutes for events such as assembly, the curriculum content of which is often so diverse as to render it accountable only to social/moral/ethical education incorporated with religious education.

As can be seen from the evidence of an 'average' day, language and maths are somewhat over-represented at the expense of technology, the humanities, arts, and PE. However, if one then reviews these proportions over the course of a whole week when, for example, children were taken out for an environmental walk (humanities), had an opportunity on two half-days to use the computer for problem solving (technology), made stable but tall structures in relation to the topic of their walk (science/technology/design), and had further opportunities for drama and painting also as a result of the topic – all this mainly emanating from language/maths time – then balance becomes more representative. While not all of the planning was matched exactly by practice (for like all good early childhood educators the students applied a desirable flexibility whenever appropriate), the deviation from it was quite small. What it reveals is something not that far from National Curriculum implications *and* the children were given good opportunities for a variety of play-based activities.

In the light of this, one might suggest that teachers themselves could well apply the same analysis to their own planning and implementation, for it is clear that teachers must adjust to a sharper curriculum focus than perhaps has occurred in the past. One of the difficulties, of course, is the question of how we define what we do, e.g. a cooking activity with young children is most decidedly 'science' as are a majority of activities provided within sand and water play. If, like the students, adults in the classroom committed more of this kind of planning to paper, for a while at least, it would be relatively easy to 'label' activities under National Curriculum terms. In doing this, teachers might find that there is in fact more time for 'extras' than they believed, something which could add significantly to the

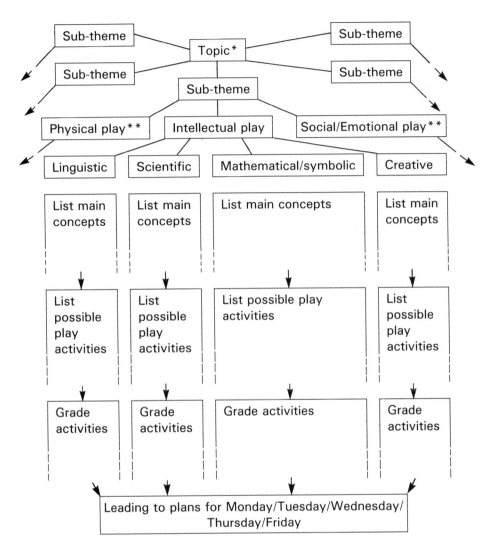

*A single topic usually lends itself to identification of certain sub-themes all of which may be identified or particular individual ones become the main topic of focus themselves. If sub-themes are not identified this can lead to topic activities becoming very superficial and lacking focus.

**The headings used in Fig. 1.1 should be added below each of these main headings as with intellectual play.

Fig. 6.1. An organizational framework for play activities within a topic-based approach. Note that this model is better drawn on a very large sheet of paper or a concertina sheet for each area.

breadth, balance, relevance and differentiation of any curriculum for all children. Figure 6.1 indicates a way in which this kind of planning can be formulated and expanded according to teachers' needs.

A few extra points about topics need mentioning. If we are trying to develop independence and autonomy in children it is no good planning knowledge-based topics through which children will need to be dependent on the teacher. Young children cannot know anything of 'The Romans' and will need to be spoon-fed information. Such topics are unhelpful to everyone concerned, whereas topics on sounds, families, happiness and colour, for example, will allow personal contributions from teachers and children alike.

The greatest conflict lies elsewhere: none of this analysis of curriculum content planning says anything about the effectiveness of different teaching and learning situations or where the similarities and differences lie. Nor does it show the amount of time spent by individual children on the various activities. Most importantly, it does not suggest much about the quality of what is being done by the children or provided by the teachers in implementing the curriculum. This must come from whole-school and individual teacher evaluations which are explored more fully in Wragg (1987) and Moyles (1988).

Implementing the curriculum: organizing for learning

It is evident in committing anything to paper as above that it connotes an unacceptable didacticism, just as the National Curriculum document itself appears to do. Putting aims to philosophies of education is notoriously difficult. Readers may well be heard to say 'Whatever happened to play?' As already intimated, play is a process on the way to learning, albeit a vital and impressionable one, and it is within implementing the curriculum itself that play, as defined earlier in this book, comes into its own, for it is in the development of many of the intangibles that play excels. Attitudes, motivation, perseverance, concentration, cooperation, reflection, autonomy and enjoyment in being a learner are some of the features of the curriculum which cannot be determined within subject boundaries. They permeate a whole view of learning which is not possible to determine within a defined statement of content, yet it is these areas above all which determine what and how a young child will learn.

Children exhibit all these traits in their play, particularly if adult providers are clear in their own minds what different play opportunities actually provide for children in terms of learning. To play effectively, children need:

- playmates, play spaces or areas, play materials, play time, play to be valued by those around them;

- opportunities to play in pairs, in small groups, alone, alongside others, with adults;
- time for exploring through language what they have done and how they can describe the experience;
- time to follow through what they begin (so often time is not made for this and much valuable work is left unfinished and uncherished);
- experiences to broaden and deepen what they know already and what they can already do;
- stimulation and encouragement to do and learn more; and
- planned and spontaneous play opportunities.

Each of these must be accounted for within the classroom environment and, as often as possible, outside too. Let us take another playing and learning situation and explore it in the light of all the foregoing and use it as a basis for then reflecting on classroom organization and management.

The class is made up of 28 five- and 6-year-old middle infants, who come from a range of backgrounds. The classroom is arranged in roughly five areas as follows:

1. A carpet area, basically for whole-class and larger-group activities and it also houses a whole range of materials for language including, at this time, a computer with a word-processing facility.
2. A pretend/imaginative play area which is sometimes a home corner and sometimes different kinds of shops and services.
3. An investigation area for group work for science and maths activities which contains a whole range of materials including sand and water, constructional toys, sorting boxes, and so on.
4. Next to (3) is a 'creative' area where all materials for art, craft and design activities are housed – junk modelling materials, glue, scissors, etc.
5. A 'stimulus' area where topic materials are displayed and used and children can display themselves things of interest which they wish to 'show and tell' others.

Classroom tables and chairs are arranged in groups within these areas and the organization of the whole classroom is shown in Fig. 6.2. The theme of current interest is 'Dark and Light', and the story of *The Iron Man*, by Ted Hughes, is being read to the class as an integral part of the topic. The teacher feels strongly that each day should begin as far as possible where the previous one ended, in order that children should understand the temporal nature of events and should be able to link past, present and future actions naturally. As on any day, in any class, there are children who still have work in progress, who are ready to move on to new activities, who need to practise what they have nearly mastered, and who have individual needs which should be met. On this particular day, two older children from the juniors are coming into the class to help with the computer activities; the ancillary helper works with this class in the morning and a parent helps in the afternoon.

Discussion with the children the previous day resulted in the teacher planning the following activities, the materials for which have been put out prior to the children arriving or are where the children know they can find them:

1. Making chocolate and vanilla biscuits so that six children can explore dark and light in another context (investigation area). The ancillary will be in charge of this activity. She already has a recipe to discuss with the children, and the children are bringing small sums of money and the first task will be to decide on the necessary ingredients and to go shopping for them.
2. Stories to be written about the Iron Man on the computer – three children have to finish theirs and two others want to start a story (language area). Words associated with the story have been put into the

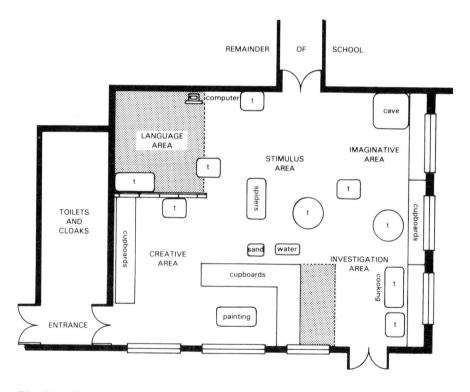

Fig. 6.2. Plan of the classroom layout and organization.

memory of the word-processing programme so that the children have an immediate word bank readily available to them. Children who wrote their stories yesterday will need time to read them to others to enhance their own competence and stimulate other children to try their own stories when the opportunity arises. The juniors will help the finishers and those wanting to start.

3. Five children who earlier in the week had made Iron Man junk models, are writing a 'How to' book for the rest of the class (language area). This they will need to try to finish and they will also need time to show and talk to the others about it.

4. Six children started exploring 'dark to light' paint mixing yesterday, beginning with a dark colour such as dark blue and gradually adding white until the colour they achieved was almost white (creative area). Some have painted this into stripes on the page, others have randomly swirled the colours on to paper. The teacher feels it would be interesting for them to concentrate today on making concentric patterns with the paints which will give a kind of 'black hole' effect and reinforce work previously done by the class on circular shapes. She has provided circular paper and will first let the children explore what they might do with this before she directs them into the concentric circle idea.

5. Several of the children expressed an interest in making a dark cave in the classroom yesterday and the teacher has already made a start on the pretend/imaginative area by bringing in some pieces of dark material and a role of stone-faced wallpaper. Some children have said they will bring in large pieces of polystyrene and cardboard boxes today to make rocks and walls. The teacher has ensured that there is plenty of black and white paint available (some ready-mixed, some dry) when needed.

6. Two black spiders found by the children yesterday are housed in a plastic tank on the stimulus table. They appear to have made webs in two of the corners and the hand lenses and miniscopes which the children asked for yesterday have now been borrowed from the science stock cupboard and are available for the children's use. The teacher feels sure that Bhavin and Pritesh (two of her 'livelier' boys) will be motivated to draw the spiders today and perhaps to find out more about them. She has checked that the school library has plenty of simple books on spiders and perhaps the boys will be interested to find some during today or tomorrow.

7. At 11.20 the class has a hall time and today the teacher will continue exploration of 'light' feelings and 'dark' feelings. It was surprising last week how Rita and Nicki (never leaders at the best of times) led other children in developing these moods. Perhaps others will 'shine' today, though hopefully Rita and Nicki will continue to gain confidence by taking a leading role.

8. The next part of the Iron Man story will be read at the beginning of the afternoon so that the afternoon has a quiet but exciting start, which may motivate some more children to try story writing. As the juniors will not be available this afternoon, those children who have already finished their stories will perhaps be encouraged to help those who are just beginning.

The day starts with the children arriving roughly together, they 'register' themselves by placing their cardboard mounted 'person' in the appropriate set for 'Dinners', 'Going Home', 'Having Sandwiches'. Those who have brought items for the cave take them straight to the prepared area. Several children want to get straight on with their activities from yesterday and the teacher asks those who are unsure what to do to talk together, on the carpet, about what they would like to do while she deals with the necessary administration and checks that those children who are already underway with their activities know what they are doing. The computer group are discussing suitable words to use when the juniors arrive. The teacher returns to the children on the carpet, selects a group of six from those who wish to cook with the ancillary which leaves her with seven children. The two boys, as she had guessed, are really keen to explore the spiders. The teacher asks them to think what they might like to do about spiders. One of the remaining children decides she would like to join the boys, leaving four to work on the construction of the cave with the teacher. The teacher suggests to the children wanting to make the cave that they draw some designs to show how they would like it to look. They go off to get paper and crayons and can shortly be seen measuring out the area in strides with a metre rule and pieces of string, and they appear to have split into pairs. This should lead to some good discussion later. The three 'spider' children have decided that they, too, want to draw and they fetch their own materials and seat themselves round the stimulus table. It is now 9.25 a.m. The teacher begins to circulate around the room discussing with the children what they are doing, getting them to explain activities to her and other children. As the first group of story writers finish, they talk with the teacher and the prospective story writers about their own efforts, the difficulties and possibilities, and what the juniors did to help! They then go off to mount their stories (one has suggested that this should be on silver foil) and the new story writers move to their task. The spider group have now begun to argue about how many legs a spider has. The teacher joins them to talk to them about it and eventually asks how they might find out what they want to know. The spiders are put into minispectors *and* inspected with hand lenses as well. Still no agreement. Then Bhavin suggests fetching a book. The teacher makes a note on her pad to perhaps talk to them about 'eight' tomorrow.

The role of the teacher throughout is to support what the children

Plate 9. Adults must talk to children about their learning.

themselves are keen to learn and interested in approaching. Some of this support is provided long before they arrive in the form of material preparation, e.g. the circular paper for the 'painters', the science equipment for the stimulus area, the materials for the pretend/imaginative area. She has also prepared back-up materials in the form of duplicated sheets, directed play suggestions with particular materials, and selected some games pertinent to the topic which children can choose from the 'I don't know what to do box' (rarely used, incidentally, in this classroom!). A description of her day could proceed *ad infinitum*, as she moves from group to group, listening, occasionally questioning, making suggestions, commenting on the quality of what children are doing, recommending different courses of action and, all the time, valuing what the children are doing, which is essentially based in the process of play and noting different children's responses and likely future needs. Sufficient emphasis cannot be given to the teacher attaching considerable value to such play activities as those described above and sometimes being a part of it. For example, the cave designers eventually could not agree on what their representation should be like despite quite accurate measurements and use of space and imagination. They decided in discussion with the teacher to let the other children vote for the design of their choice and abide by the result. This negotiation is a vital part of the *social* nature of classroom life and moral issues of choice and responsibility, and can be seen occurring quite frequently in this type of classroom. It would be possible to devote a whole book to exploring the variety of opportunities (and perhaps missed opportunities) available to the teacher and the children in the above classroom organization and implementation.

What is clear within this type of class management is the need for teachers to monitor what the children actually do and how they do it. They need to observe, record and assess learning and all associated attitudes in the ways previously discussed. Adults must talk to children about their learning if they are to find out about it themselves for, as has already been noted, the products of children's learning are not always the best guides to what has been learned and the quality of that learning. It is to this notion, then, that attention is turned in the next chapter.

7

Play and Progress: Observing, Recording and Assessing the Value of Play

Scenario

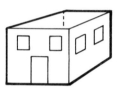

1. Beth, aged 6 years and 8 months, has made a clay house something like that shown above. She had decided earlier that the house needed a roof and is now working at the clay table in a group of eight children who are all at various stages in the construction of their houses. Beth manipulates her piece of clay for 6 or 7 minutes, apparently aimlessly and unsure of her procedure, though her face has a rather intent look and she ignores attempts at conversation by her nearest peer. The teacher arrives at Beth's side and asks why she has not started:

> **Teacher:** Are you going to cut some rectangles for your roof? How are you going to do it?
> **Beth:** Triangles. I want triangles.
> **Teacher:** Come along then, cut some rectangles or you won't get finished today.

(The teacher appears to assume that Beth has simply misunderstood the terminology.)

Beth continues to stare at her lump of clay and eventually pushes it down hard with her hand. She then calls out for a rolling pin which, when she fails to gain a response, she grabs from the next child. He appears not to be too concerned and Beth carefully rolls the clay into an oval shape.

She tells her neighbour what she is doing but he appears to be too involved with his own house to concern himself. She then fetches a clay modelling tool, stares intently at her house and inscribes a large equilateral triangle in the clay. She proceeds to cut it out and holds it up over one side edge of the cubic house. The teacher notices and comes to Beth saying: 'Well, that's a very good idea. What are you going to do now?' The child explains that she will cut some more triangles and fit them together.

Teacher: How many will you need?
Beth: Two.
Teacher: Are you sure its two? How many sides does your house have – two or four?
Beth: Four, but I need two triangles.
Teacher: Well carry on and we'll see what happens.

Beth does carry on and cuts a further triangle, using the first one as a template, which she props opposite the original on the other side of the house. She looks at her model and prompts the boy next to her: 'Hey. Look at my roof!' Unimpressed, he suggests: 'It's got holes what'll let the rain in!' Beth looks at her remnants of clay, forms them into a ball again and then rolls out a flat shape from which she cuts a smaller triangle than the previous two, using this one to cut a second small triangle. She then balances one at each end of the roof thus making a pyramid shape. She calls for the teacher who compliments her on her good construction and suggests that slip is now all that is required to fix it all together.

The total time taken up to this point is 45 minutes. Beth continues to work on her roof for a further 40 minutes until she is obviously very satisfied with it. She wants to show it to the other children but the teacher insists there is not time today. Beth puts her model on a table as instructed and goes to read a book.

It is often very difficult indeed to actually see progression within play situations and this is, no doubt, one of the many reasons why tangible evidence of progress in the form of writing or number work appears to have so much greater status for many adults. Yet progress is indeed being made in the above scene if only we are prepared to observe closely what Beth was doing and give her the time to think things through herself, in this case nearly an entire afternoon. Documenting that progress, however, is not an easy task. As Millar (1968:246) suggests: 'The young are relatively slow to digest information returned from explorations and the time they need can easily be underestimated.' Teachers must, of course, be able to recognize different aspects of progress in the children they teach, not only in the name of accountability but for their own professional satisfaction. If play is to be provided in the classroom in ways already suggested then adults must become adept at assessing, observing, monitoring and recording what occurs through play activities and provide the necessary resources, for it is only by knowing where children are now that we can ensure progress and understanding when it occurs.

The problem appears to be that human beings are all unique and all perceive situations in different ways depending upon their own experiences, expectations, attitudes and values and, therefore, interpretation of what individuals observe and what they assess as progress will be different from person to person as we each operate our own selection systems. If one adds to this the known mismatches between children's and teachers' understandings and expectations of classroom life interactions (Bennett, 1976), the potential difficulties are compounded even further. As Armstrong (1980:206) states: 'How are we to understand the understanding of children? One way of beginning is to examine, with careful sympathy, the thought and action of the children whom we ourselves are teaching.'

All teachers are capable of spontaneous acts of observation, mental and written note-taking and continuous assessment of a situation: they do it all the time as their constant comments and even facial and bodily expressions towards children in the classroom context show! Although the reader can only respond to the written account in the scenario above and personal observation in the classroom would be preferable, it is possible to get a 'feel' for this child's actions, intentions, interactions and progress. The fact that each individual will interpret the situation differently will become apparent if, as an example, a reader notes their own individual and independent response to the clay episode under the following headings:

- Child's activity;
- Attitude to the task;
- Self-initiation and responsibility;
- Learning – concepts, skills, processes;
- Application of earlier learning;
- Communication;
- Cooperative learning; and
- Teacher intervention.

The notes made might then be compared with those of a colleague who has undertaken a similar activity independently. It is highly likely that the two teachers will agree on less than half the points. In fact, my own interpretation of the situation may well be contended by readers! There will be necessary qualifications of aspects and features and, inevitably, some discussion on terminology, e.g. what exactly is meant by a 'concept' or 'cooperative learning'? Am I accurate in suggesting the teacher's apparent dismissal of Beth's word 'triangle' rather than 'rectangle'?

Considered from another angle, how far can we apply Bennett *et al.*'s (1984) model of learning as discussed in Chapter 2? A very general and brief analysis might be:

1. **Incremental tasks.** Beth is reproducing her ideas on clay structures from her previous experience of making the house. She had presumably been taught the techniques of using the medium at an earlier date.
2. **Restructuring tasks.** In the first part of the model she was required to form squares and mount these into a cubic structure. She is now looking afresh at using the medium to form quite a different, pyramidal structure but still using established skills to flatten the clay, the shape and thickness being of her own choosing.
3. **Enrichment tasks.** Her apparent belief that two triangles will be sufficient to cover the roof shows that she is trying to apply earlier learning to a new situation. She then discovers the need for four triangles and, conceptually, is well on the way to establishing the notion of three-dimensional structuring from flat clay shapes.
4. **Practice skills.** She is maintaining skills and repeating several processes discovered in previous sessions with the clay and, once the need for two extra triangles is discovered, she is able to apply her previous knowledge and skills rapidly.
5. **Revision.** Using the clay a further time has helped Beth to revise her earlier understanding of its properties, texture and the demands of the medium.

Whether one considers this account to be accurate and acceptable will be determined by the views formulated in examining the contents of the scenario and, again, could well vary if two independent readers compare their own thoughts.

In terms of observing children at play the kind of discrepancies which will have appeared between the two readers and the writer and readers' interpretations of the same situation, have very radical implications for the teacher. Making open and unstructured observational notes of a child at play will generate a plethora of information regarding development, progress, attitude, sociability, and so on, but a great deal of this will never be analysed into a useful form due to its sheer quantity and lack of structure. It is extremely important to decide what one wants to observe before observing, partly because this is economical of time but more because the activity will gain greater purpose and be likely to yield more useful information about children and their progress. There is, of course, the danger that people will see only what they want to see if this is highly predetermined and, among others, King (1978) and Desforges and Cockburn (1988) clearly show that this can occur. It is, however, crucial that teachers and others are really clear about their fundamental aims and learning objectives for children in play situations because, without such clarity, how do we know what it is we are looking for? Moreover, how do we justify our work to others without being able to provide evidence from observations, data collection and our own assessments of the value of play? Is there a time when playing is not learning? We will only know this if we thoroughly understand the responses of the children to the activities and tasks provided for them. Kalverboer (1977:121) states clearly from his research that:

> play contains crucial information about a child's developmental level, his organizing capacities and his emotional state. To make this information available, categorization and measurement are necessary.

What is required is an acceptance by teachers and others that some play in the classroom is created for children simply to have fun and relaxation. Teachers must ask themselves (and answer truthfully!): 'What is the purpose of this play?' If the honest answer is to keep the children quietly occupied while the teacher proceeds with directed group work, then so be it, but the danger lies in teachers fooling themselves regarding learning expectations and outcomes, particularly in relation to play. If the play is intended to have a learning outcome then the question must be 'What?' – and what direction is required, if any at this stage, from the teacher? But learning outcomes are highly dependent upon the child's current state of development and maturity and their present ability to cope with different aspects of school life which, as discussed in earlier chapters, offer different expectations and make different requirements on children from the home background. As Holdaway implies, teachers with their professional expertise and knowledge need to justify their decisions, considering that:

> Developmental learning ... is ... regulated and paced by the learner in response to inner controls of a highly sensitive nature.... This regulation system may decree, for instance, a period of regression to a lower stage – something which would seldom be predicted or required by the progress-oriented adult. (Holdaway, 1979:47)

The play spiral model takes regression and progression in its stride and Bennett *et al.*'s (1984) model of learning incorporates practice and revision within its framework. The early years curriculum provides the base from which this will operate and it is to this we now return.

Aims and objectives for the curriculum

Within the broader framework of the local education authority's and school's policies and guidelines, teachers normally have the responsibility to make all necessary provision for their own class of children. This is a strength of the British system (Davis *et al.*, 1986) and determines a high level of responsibility for the teacher. Play is both a process and mode which can be operated within the normal curriculum and what must be reiterated is that *play is not a curriculum in itself*, as was noted in Chapter 6. Although children need a *knowledge* of the play materials, their functions, properties and names, and require *skills* of manipulation and coordination in handling them, play is a means by which children engage in different aspects of the curriculum towards learning. We must observe, assess and record play in whatever 'area' children are currently involved and at whatever stage they are in their development.

Kerry and Tollitt (1987) firmly believe that early years teachers should reject the notion of a subject curriculum in favour of a conceptually based one, and argue that teachers find it easier to 'question "What shall I do with the children?" than to explore the problem "What concepts/skills do my five/six/seven year olds need to acquire this year...?" ' (Kerry and Tollitt, 1987:121). While I feel great empathy with this view, a National Curriculum is now a reality and applicable to 5-year-olds upwards, as well as implicitly encompassing the education of 4-year-olds in reception classes. Early years teachers must consider procedures for implementing an integrated curriculum (much favoured by HMI in many reports), integrated by including the development of the whole child, a conceptual framework for early learning and a view of the range of possible subjects which can be incorporated.

Assuming, as previously, that a topic approach is adopted by early years teachers, they must ask themselves certain questions before they even begin to make provision for play and learning:

- What am I going to provide?
- Why am I making this particular provision?
- Where will the children be starting from? Will this topic require children to restructure and enrich their knowledge as well as provide practice and revision of previously learned skills?
- How far do my plans fit in with the school's requirements?
- What concepts form the basis of my topic?
- What skills do I hope the children will acquire?
- What curriculum areas will it be feasible to cover?
- What will my approach be: tasks, activities, free play/directed play ...?
- What resource provision will I need to make?
- Do I know and understand these resources myself?
- How will the classroom need to be organized?
- What about the individual needs within my class?
- Will what I want to do really interest, stimulate and motivate these children?

- How will I monitor and assess what individuals are doing and learning and their attitudes to tasks?
- What observations will I undertake of individuals, groups, the class ...?
- What records will I need to keep?

The wealth of information provided by even brief notes in answer to these questions, will serve to establish and determine several crucial factors in relation to the assessment, observation and recording of what children actually do and learn and the progress made. A few other factors deserve mention before examining a concept of progress and its relationships to these three areas.

Woodhead (1988) reminds us that children have their own priorities for learning: the sensitive teacher who knows her class will be alert to this potential, particularly through children's play, and will be ready to take account of it within the planning. It is necessary, too, to remember and be aware of the fact that children can be involved during play in deep mental

Plate 10. Children can be involved during play in deep mental processes which are taxing of energy.

processes which are taxing of energy. A teacher's request to do some 'work' could provide both real frustration and another very demanding mental task. All children, like adults, need opportunities to rest between stretches of mental activity, and this can simply be by relaxing by sitting down or, more likely, by letting off steam and engaging in some gross physical activity. Early years teachers really do have to plan for everything!

Remaining objective is sometimes quite difficult. Different classes produce and induce different emotions in the teacher. Sometimes the class begins the year with a delightful sense of cohesion and social conscience – in other years the children are highly individual in their approach to play and tasks, and cooperative learning does not come easily. Then again, in some years groups form themselves into peer group play arrangements for good or ill! At these times, it is even more important to remain calm and analytical and attempt to itemize and interpret what happens.

Knowing your resources, especially play materials, is of vital importance. What do they really provide for the children? Are you aware enough yourself of the potential of each resource? Do you have insights into directing more challenging play with them? Kirklees Guidelines for Nursery Education (1985) contain a list of fairly typical play materials and resources which were analysed by teachers to discover the main development and learning potential within each of them under what might be described as developmental categories. This provides an excellent starting point for teachers and others who need a guide to develop a similar list for their own resource provision. Students on teaching practice have been persuaded to analyse both materials and activities by use of a checklist similar to the one shown in Fig. 7.1, and are always amazed by the richness and variety provided by even simple resources for children's learning, once the adults themselves have such knowledge.

Finally, children need time, not only to think through their problems (Beth spent much time on this process) but also to formulate their own questions and commit information to memory. Research undertaken by Turnure *et al.* (1976) found that children who formulated their own questions about objects were able to recall three times as many items, on a subsequent test, compared with those children who were only given information about the objects in a variety of ways. In relation to traditional teaching and learning this has vast implications. For, as suggested by Almy (1977:206):

> The teacher in the traditional classroom spends much time *telling* the children about the world and then questioning them as to whether they have remembered what they have been told. Piagetian theory seems to call for a teacher who listens more.

What? – State material activity ....

Who? – State age group of children ....

         Number of children ....

What purpose? – Evaluator should state possible objectives/potential regarding children's development/learning, including likely influence on all or some of the following:

Social – communication (verbal/non-verbal)
        – friendship
        – sharing and turn-taking
        – cooperation
        – role play ....

Intellectual – concepts
          – ideas
          – thinking ability, reasoning, curiosity
          – decision making/problem solving
          – facts/knowledge

          ....

Physical/psychomotor – fine/gross
                  – manipulation
                  – coordination
                  – spatial awareness ....

Emotional/moral – personal responses of children
              – control of emotions
              – sensitivity to others
              – self-concept
              – enjoyment
              – care and respect for materials

          ....

Aesthetic – creative ability
        – shape and form
        – expressive ability

Attitude/motivation ....

Individuality/personality ....

Behaviour ....

Opportunities for cognitive challenge generally ....

....

Concentration ....

Potential difficulties in use/storage ....

Fig. 7.1. Evaluation of materials and activities for play.

Progress

This is something frequently talked about but rarely specified! The *Oxford Dictionary* defines progress as 'to advance or develop, especially to a better state'. Perhaps in children's progression 'better state' needs to be interpreted as rather more an 'experienced state' which, in itself, encourages the development of more concepts, knowledge, skills, and so on.

The word progress, however defined, usually represents something of a blanket terminology and it is helpful in the first instance to think of progress within long- and short-term aims. Children will, in the long term, make *developmental* progress. Just as they have learned to walk and talk over periods of approximately 1 and 2 years respectively, so they will continue to develop, mature and grow physically within a normal environment. Other than normal bodily and emotional requirements, little needs to be done to promote this kind of progress. When it comes to *skills* many of these are related to development, but skills such as using scissors can and will need to be taught, and they can be learned in a relatively short time. Adults must not be afraid of helping children to learn many different techniques, skills and processes which, once mastered, can help other learning, particularly that of independence.

In school, adults must bear in mind the child's overall developmental progress, but most of all they must expect progress in relation to what is actually taught and accept that children will not learn all necessary and useful skills without someone to teach them. Having been taught, progress can then be determined in relation to the application of knowledge and skills. In the context of Beth's experience with the clay, she had previously been taught the skills of wedging, rolling and cutting the clay. Progress is evident in the fact that she then used these skills spontaneously to further her construction. In addition, she had previously been taught the spatial concepts of square, triangle and rectangle, and had applied this knowledge to house and roof forms selectively. She had learned the properties of the clay through the experience of using it herself. The final point needs emphasis: young children gain experiences and learn from what they themselves handle and absorb first hand. The play spiral takes account of this and necessary teaching in the form of directing play activities at certain points. The important consideration is that children have optimum times when skills need to be taught and these can only be determined by having a knowledge of individuals supported by observation of the child 'in action'.

In a normal school year of approximately 9 months, it could be expected that children between 4 and 8 years of age will make developmental progress appropriate to their age and stage in relation to:

• physical growth;

- growth in gross and fine motor skills;
- growth of intelligence (including concepts, knowledge, understandings, skills, e.g. problem solving, and processes);
- growth of self-concept and personal skills;
- growth of perceptual skills;
- growth in creativity;
- growth in social skills and growing independence;
- growth in general life experiences and school skills, such as persistence and concentration;
- growth of morality;
- growth in communication skills; and
- growth in emotional stability.

There are many helpful and thorough texts which provide a breakdown of these generalized developmental aspects which provide an excellent framework for those wishing to gain a more detailed insight (see Gessell *et al.*, 1973; Curtis and Wignall, 1981; Bee, 1985). In addition, the contents of several tests identified by Bate *et al.* (1982) give useful information about what psychologists and others have felt it suitable and practical to assess and record in relation to the developing child. It is not suggested that teachers use the tests as such but merely consult the detailed contents. Some developmental traits will be obvious, such as physical growth in height and girth. Others will be less obvious without a close look every now and again at the individuals within the class.

Shorter-term progress will inevitably relate to the development of more specific and detailed skills and information being absorbed. The example in Fig. 7.2, given in class matrix format, will serve to explain, within the topic of spiders, the links between the long- and short-term aims refined eventually into children's activities.

Individual teachers may actually find it quite difficult, especially if they have had the same age group for a few years, to specify progress over the 4- or 5-year span of first school education. For this reason, it is advisable that the whole staff decide together on both the potential of a topic and the potential of individual resources and activities wherever possible. This can be done periodically, especially if they are familiar with a whole-school topic approach, where they get together to brainstorm concepts, knowledge, skills, and so on. The same principles can be applied to resources; thus, hopefully, modifying the effect of what has been called 'the tadpole syndrome', the situation where children are exposed to spawn, tadpoles and developing frogs every year from the age of 3 without any consideration of what incrementally should be emphasized at each age. Children love tadpoles but their knowledge does not increase simply because they have increased in age and maturity. Teachers must contemplate what understandings each new year will make possible. A simple diagrammatic way of

Concepts/skills/processes															
Children	Concept 1 Fear	Skill 1 Handling gently	Skill 1a Learning characteristics	Process 1 Observation	Process 1a Explaining	Concept 2 Black	Skill 2 Observation drawing	Skill 2a Colour mixing	Process 2 Comparison	Process 2a Prediction	Concept 3 Webs	Skill 3 Weaving	Skill 3a Interweaving movements	Process 3 Interpretation	Process 3a Improvization
Child A															
Child B															
Child C															
Child D															
......															
......															

Fig. 7.2. Class matrix to plot concept/skill development within a topic on spiders. Overlap again exists between concepts, processes and skills and those areas chosen for recording will relate, to a certain extent, to personal choice, though will remain within boundaries all teachers will understand. A more detailed list is likely to be part of the planning as explored in Fig. 6.1.

The identified concepts, skills and processes will form a long or short list dependent upon the length of time over which the matrix will be used. Teachers might find it helpful to identify, in the first instance, all those possible within a topic and then have smaller matrices which tend to be more manageable in the classroom.

plotting progress in topic items or resources is given in Fig. 7.3. An example of a sheet for evaluation of materials and activities is given in Fig. 7.1.

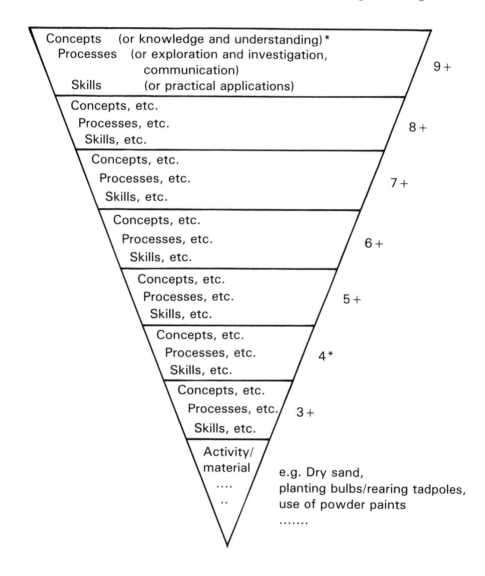

Fig. 7.3. A view of progression. Note that it is vitally important that learning, in any area, is introduced to children at the optimum time within their development, experiences and understanding. *The 5–16 Guidelines for Maths and Science within the National Curriculum will be particularly helpful in this regard.

Making observations

Teachers are very good at knowing generally what is happening within their classrooms, who is doing what, with whom, and so on, fairly intuitively. But intuitive knowledge gives only a limited understanding of the classroom situation and needs to be supported by accurate observation and further investigation if the needs, expectations and learning requirements of individuals are to be understood fully.

Teachers must not feel guilty about the time they spend standing back, observing and reflecting on what is happening in their classrooms. It is a vital part of their role and one which is rarely exploited to the full by early years teachers who feel that they must be totally involved, constantly. This often leads to teachers having only fleeting functional and organizational interactions with children which frequently result in the learning of small groups and individuals going unrecognized. Children will let teachers and other adults pursue their own tasks provided

1. The classroom management and organization is sound and encourages autonomy.
2. The activities provided are interesting and appropriate to the children's needs.
3. They know and expect that the adults will distance themselves occasionally.
4. The adult indicates clearly by a certain signal (carrying a particular note pad, wearing a badge or hat) that he or she is unavailable for comment.

Observations can be undertaken in several different ways for a range of purposes and the most useful ones for early childhood personnel are given in Table 7.1.

What to observe

Particularly in nursery classrooms where a whole range of play resources and activities are prepared for the children subsequent to their arrival, one basic piece of information the teacher needs to know is *what* a child played with in any session or day. Even in the more structured infant or first school classroom, appropriate choice for the children requires their chosen activities to be monitored. This can easily be made the responsibility of the child through a name tag system, which involves children having a set of their own name cards (possibly duplicated well in advance) and having pockets allocated and mounted in a suitable place and into which children put one of their name cards for each activity they undertake. Another useful system is that of ticking off names/picture cues on a list provided in close proximity to the equipment, e.g. the sheet could be attached to the

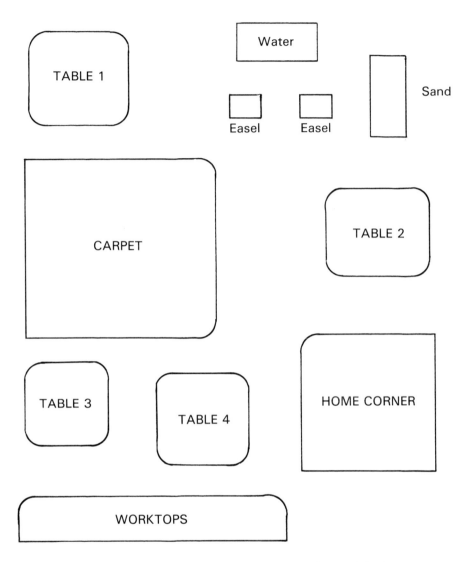

Fig. 7.4. Classroom table plan for noting activities, child participation or both.

side of the playhouse or a card could be provided with the box of construction materials and children tick or cross off their names when they have undertaken that particular activity. The adults themselves might also monitor who does what by having duplicated layout plans of the classroom arrangement and resources, such as that shown in Fig. 7.4, and recording during the day which children are where, doing what. This has the advantage of highlighting those children who pursued one or two activities and those who constantly changed their activities.

Table 7.1. Some useful methods and objectives for making classroom observations. Note that some objectives may require the teacher to set expectations as is normally the case in research projects (see Croll, 1984: Ch. 2), which will determine in detail what exactly it is they wish to observe.

Type of observation	*Main objectives*
General, visual 'sweep'	Get a feel for the way the class operates as a unit. Indicate whether resources and areas are appropriate to the children's working needs. Look for isolated children, and events likely to cause disruption. This can be done through *time sampling*, i.e. undertaking this kind of sweep at predetermined time intervals
Total class scanning	To find out what all the members of the class are doing or to count how many are engaged in particular activities. This can again be operated at timed intervals
Time-of-day scan	To find out, for example, how children enter and leave the classroom, organize themselves for dinner time, PE, the teacher noting the particular events which occur at specified times. This is also useful at the end of the day to find out how effectively the children have tidied their drawers and working spaces and left cloakroom facilities, etc.
Single activity in progress	Find out if activity is popular, with whom, for how long, motivation and concentration, and child–child interaction prompted by the activity. Assess how children approach the activity and if any reject it on sight. This can be continuously recorded or time sampled
Single child, single activity	Close observation of one child and his/her exhibited understanding and needs in one particular classroom activity. What distractions, interruptions occurred for the child, was the play of good quality, how did it end? Did child talk to him/herself, with others, what quality was inherent in the play?

Type of observation	Main objectives
Single child throughout many activities and situations	Follow child, either constantly or at timed intervals (choice of time will depend on what the teacher wishes to find out), to assess behaviour, concentration, interactions, tasks achieved in any one day or week
Group of children in a single activity	Observe to see how the children interact with each other. Do they work cooperatively, individually, independently? What language is used, by whom, for how long? How on-task is the group?
Friendship groups	Note by scanning the whole range of activities who is involved with whom. Are these friendships sustained over a number of activities or specific to one or two? Are they sustained over a period of time or merely occur within one day/session?
Particular concepts or skills being exhibited	Observe an activity or series of activities in which children are likely to exhibit a particular concept or skill and note the individuals for record purposes
Specific behaviour being evidenced	Find out when moments of disruption occur in the classroom. Who is directly involved, indirectly involved? At what time and in what context did the disruption occur? How was it resolved – by a child, teacher, other adult?
Adults in the classroom	To find out how often and in what ways the adult interacts and intervenes in children's activities. What was the quality of this? How did the adult approach – by invitation, interruption? Was the adult part of the play, peripheral to the play?

Knowing what has been attempted is quite important for those children who are exhibiting a tendency to stick to one type of activity at the expense of others and the learning they can provide. (Occasionally, children, for emotional reasons, will persist in certain activities and this will be discussed in Chapter 8.) It is also important to know *how* the child played – socially, with whom – and what their attitudes and motivations appeared to be. What the child actually did and what he or she achieved through that particular play activity (e.g. new skills, mastery of old ones, communication, enjoyment, persistence), can be taken into account when developing observation schedules. In terms of progress, the vital questions then become where might the child go from here, what do they now need to learn, can this be achieved through directed play, what else does the child need, where do we go from here – revision, practice, or more of the same? For as Brierley (1987:22) suggests: 'Skills are first learned slowly and by repetition. After becoming fully established, they acquire a pattern, unique to the person, the striking characteristic of which is its durability.'

The quality of children's play, tasks and learning is of vital importance. This can be monitored by keeping constantly in mind the curriculum principles explored earlier in this chapter and in the previous one and reviewing what is happening through frequent observations with specific checklists. As has already been emphasized, it is necessary to understand both resource and task provision and their effects on learning. Observations might also include reflecting on the answers to the following:

1. Which resources and activities:
   - are used most frequently at present and why is this?
   - encourage extended bouts of play and concentration?
   - encourage independence and autonomy in children?
   - encourage children to talk (a) with peers and (b) with adults and contain sustained conversations?
   - promote most discussion of outcomes?
   - encourage cooperative play and learning?
   - encourage solitary and/or parallel play?
   - develop most effectively the skills of coordination, manipulation, imagination and creativity?
   - develop mathematical, scientific, technological, environmental, geographical, historical, religious and aesthetic understandings, values and knowledge?
   - most encourage children to elaborate upon their play, use their imaginations, skills, knowledge, solve problems with persistence and care?
   - most encourage a multi-sensory approach to learning?
   - encourage children to explore moral and ethical issues?
   - seem likely to produce most aggressive or inappropriate behaviour in children?
   - appear more popular when an adult is present or involved?
   - are most useful for specific topics?
2. Do boys and girls differ in their choice of resources and materials? What is the reason for this?

3. Do children select their own resources and activities? Can they find and return them easily?
4. Do children pursue particular ideas and transfer learning across the range of resources and activities available at any one time?

Those interested in finding out more about systematic observation, its purpose, range, advantages and disadvantages, would do well to consult Croll (1984).

Record keeping

As with progress and observation, records can be developed for a long-term view or a shorter-term view and can be records which individual teachers keep on their own work with children (shared with others or not), records of individual children or class records. Attitudes, for example, change relatively slowly, though children may in seconds master the name of a particular play material or process skill or build a model.

What adults need to clarify is the purpose of records in school and the most useful content: individual schools and authorities will determine who, basically has access to them. Table 7.2 and Table 7.3 explore why we keep records and their content and purpose, respectively.

One of the main purposes of any kind of record must be to inform teachers over the period of time in which they are concerned with a particular group of children, what actually to teach or what learning or developmental progress is likely or planned to occur. The difficulty is that it is quite possible to become totally overwhelmed by developing, completing and analysing records, time which is more usefully spent in observing children and furthering their learning. This is quite a dilemma. Moyles (1986) explains how this was resolved in her own school and, briefly, acceptable records were achieved by:

1. Detailing long-term aims and skills within the school's policies and schemes of work, which had also been prepared taking into account developmental needs.
2. Using the skills, etc., identified within particular topics undertaken by individual teachers to develop class records on a matrix system (as already indicated in Fig. 7.2).
3. Using individual profiles of children, supported by examples of specific activities, but recording only those things which were particularly noteworthy for that child ('normal' development was not recorded).

The latter item was not only supported by children's recorded work but by photographs and cassette recordings of notable activities in which the child was involved and in which real progress was evidenced. No doubt as video

Table 7.2. Record keeping: why keep individual records/profiles?

---

1. To record basic information about a child in the areas of:
   (i) intellectual ability, i.e. language, mathematics, science, problem solving, understanding concepts and processes;
   (ii) development of creativity and aesthetic awareness;
   (iii) social/moral development, attitude to work and to others;
   (iv) emotional development and independence;
   (v) physical and psychomotor development;
   (vi) health matters, handicaps, speech, vision, hearing, etc.;
   (vii) special interests and talents;
   (viii) parental involvement/attitudes
2. To record attainment/progress/difficulties/needs in a range of topics and curriculum areas
3. To monitor on-going development of individuals
4. To help the teacher to ensure that directed play and other teaching matches the needs of the individual children in her class and group effectively for particular teaching when necessary
5. To act as a guide to the child's teacher on suitable play activities and tasks for each child or group of children
6. To enable subsequent teachers to gain a better and quicker knowledge and understanding of 'new' children
7. To pass on as a cumulative and comprehensive assessment to the next phase or to agencies such as Child Welfare, Medical Officers, Child Psychologists, etc.
8. To enable the school staff, through the accumulated information on each child and class, to develop a closer knowledge and understanding of the school's needs
9. To have reliable and immediate information to pass on to a child's parents
10. To enable supply/support teachers to gain a quick knowledge of the children with whom he/she is expected to work

---

equipment becomes less expensive and simpler to operate, this will provide another vehicle.

A useful sheet for recording long-term changes is shown in Fig. 7.5 and is easily adaptable for the inclusion of other continuum possibilities readers consider necessary. It is completed by ticking or blocking in particular squares and the expectation might be that from nursery school on, completion of the boxes would follow an upward trend. Where this does not occur it is possible to make certain deductions, e.g. if a child has mixed freely in the nursery but suddenly in the first term of reception class becomes very solitary, he or she may be very unhappy in the new

Table 7.3. Record keeping: content and uses.

---

* Records must be useful in monitoring school processes and the long-term attainment, abilities and progress of individual children
* Records must help headteachers to know what is required for teaching and learning
* Records must reflect a knowledge of individual children
* Records must be easy to complete
* Records must require completion only periodically – no more than once a term gives children time to progress and develop
* Records may contain some kind of rating system or other denoting the level of the child's ability/response in certain areas.

Possible contents (in addition to those itemized in Fig. 7.3):

1. Pupil's name, address, date of birth, position in family, day-time contact, etc.
2. Personal factors, e.g. one-parent family, home background, etc., health record
3. Dates/results of assessments and tests (criterion-referenced and normative), referral to other agencies, etc.
4. Progress through pre-school experiences, playgroup, nursery, four-plus
5. Particular milestones in the child's life, i.e. new baby, death of a close relative, etc.
6. 'Open' sheets or spaces for teacher's own comments
7. Topics covered over each period of time and their main relative emphasis
8. Any official correspondence regarding this child or reports from outside agencies
9. Names/dates/teachers who have taught this child
10. Examples (named, dated and signed) of children's progress in recording

What records probably should NOT do!

Record normal progress! It is much more important to know about the child's needs now or potentially

---

situation. Similarly, a child who, at the end of the first term in the second year, suddenly changes from having good concentration to being a butterfly may have problems at home which it would be advantageous for the teacher to investigate.

Checklists are useful for itemizing likely development and learning but tend to be lengthy both to complete and consult. One of their main problems is that they are likely to detail very small steps in development, such as the ability to tie shoe laces which, although important particularly

Name of child ....   Date of birth ....

	Terms	N			Year 1			Year 2			Year 3			...
		1	2	3	1	2	3	1	2	3	1	2	3	

Social
Mixes freely
Average
Few friends
Solitary
Withdrawn

Seeks adult attention
Friendly to adults
Reserved with adults

Temperament
Very mature
Average
Immature

Good sense of humour
Average
Serious

Concentrates well
Somewhat distractible
Butterfly

Persistence
Good perseverance
Average perseverance
Labours tasks
Gives up easily

Attitude
Assured/cheerful/positive
Content and passive
Despondent

Self-reliant
Often seeks support
Dependent on peers/adults

Terms	N			Year 1			Year 2			Year 3			...
	1	2	3	1	2	3	1	2	3	1	2	3	
Learning													
Quick to learn													
Average													
Rather slow													
Very slow													
Instigates own learning													
Learns under direction													
Passive learner													
Shows real curiosity													
Cautious curiosity													
Lacks curiosity													
Powers of retention													
Good memory													
Remembers selectively													
Poor memory													
Behaviour													
Appropriately behaved													
Reasonable behaviour													
Aggressive													

Fig. 7.5. Long-term general record sheet. Note that a section on special talents and interests can also be added in order to show changes in motivation and interests. Such a section would include books/reading, writing, constructional toys, jigsaws, drawing/painting, craft/making models, sewing, music, movement, games, swimming, particular types of play, etc.

for the child's independence, tend to be symptomatic of greater physical development, fine motor skills and coordination, which should equally be manifesting themselves at around the same time, and general development could be ignored in favour of ticks against small, sometimes unrelated, skills. Other kinds of checklists are especially useful, such as those required to focus attention on specific observations, and as teachers gain more expertise in developing observations it is likely that they will refine and define their needs more clearly. The questions raised within this chapter should help teachers to gain greater clarity and definition. Shipman (1983:74) warns:

Child's name .... Robert ....   Age .... 4 years 10 months

	Rating					Comments (dated and initialled)
	1	2	3	4	5	
Motor development						
Runs confidently					✓	Loves it!
Climbs apparatus freely					✓	
Jumps over small object easily			✓			
Kicks a ball accurately			✓			
Pedals tricycle properly		✓				Poor coordination
Jumps two feet together		✓				somehow
Balances briefly on one foot	✓					
Throws a ball accurately		✓				
Sits cross-legged					✓	
Hops on one foot	✓					
Runs on tiptoe	✓					
Catches a ball – both hands		✓				–ditto–
Holds pencil/crayon correctly		✓				
Turns book one page at a time			✓			
Threads beads			✓			
Uses scissors accurately			✓			
Pours water without spillage		✓				
Builds towers of bricks				✓		And knocks them
Copies shapes accurately		✓				down!
Matches shapes correctly			✓			
Draws recognizable figures				✓		
Traces accurately			✓			
Completes up to a 25-piece jigsaw		✓				
Communication						
Listens attentively to stories					✓	
Learns songs and rhymes					✓	
Follows simple instructions					✓	
Speaks with clarity					✓	
Speaks in distinct sentences				✓		
Takes part in discussions				✓		
Defines simple objects					✓	
Matches/knows colours			✓			
Communicates with peers					✓	
Communicates with adults					✓	
Recognizes surname					✓	
Can give first and last name					✓	
Knows own address					✓	

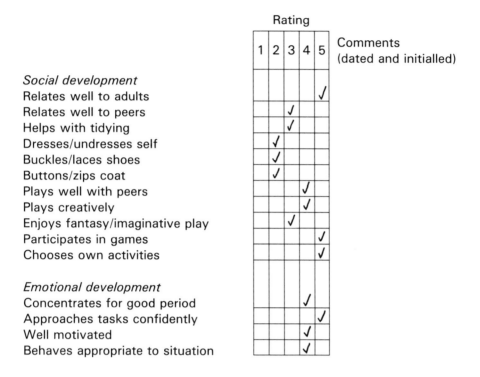

Fig. 7.6. Nursery leaving profile. On a rating scale of 1 to 5, 1 = poor through 5 = excellent.

> The time devoted to completing them [school records] is rarely matched by the time spent consulting them ... it has to be remembered that records are completed by teachers who are likely to know all about a child and interpreted later by those who do not.

The epitome of good records is brevity with clarity and depth. Teachers neither need to write everything down or have time to do so. Where cooperative efforts are made within a school's staff, it is likely that progression, development, learning and recording will be most effective. Collaboration with colleagues can also help adults significantly with assessment. As a final activity, consider the contents of the Leaver's Nursery Profile shown in Fig. 7.6, which was the first of a number of such profiles developed by one school's staff in order to give the next teacher information on individual children as an aid to his or her planning for the child's early days in the reception class. Using Table 7.4 or your own planning outline, decide how helpful this profile might be and what possible alterations, additions or modifications you would wish to make.

Table 7.4. Assessing a new child's needs.

Figure 7.6 depicts a possible profile of a child about to enter a reception class, which has been passed on by the nursery teacher

Note briefly what you would plan for this child for the first month in the reception class to promote development under the following headings (add others or make up your own if you wish!)
Language
Science
Mathematics
Creativity
Physical
Social/emotional
Topic-based learning

Then consider

1. Did you feel you had received a good, general profile of this child?
2. Was it helpful in your task?
3. Did you require more/less/different information in any category?
4. Would the inclusion of any other categories have helped you further or better?
5. Could anything have been left out of Fig. 7.6?
6. In the light of this activity what makes records truly useful in terms of (a) assessing a child's needs and (b) informing teachers of learning needs?

Assessment and testing

Most assessment in the classroom is spontaneous and impressionistic (Shipman, 1983:14). It serves the purpose of ensuring that teachers get to know the individuals reasonably well and can motivate, encourage, comment, praise, and so on, as necessary. It is only a very small sample of what children do which will be recorded for the purposes of others, such as parents, other teachers or the LEA, and this will be based on assessment. Going back to the opening scenario, what might be our assessment of Beth's progress? We can perhaps say reasonably accurately that she knows the meaning of 'triangle' and was able to use the shape effectively in her construction of the roof, therefore showing an ability for transferring knowledge from one situation to another. As no other child had considered such a roof shape, it was also evident that she was using personal creativity to solve the problem set. In relation to the play spiral, all this occurred in Beth's second and subsequent free play periods with the clay following both exploratory and directed play. As already asserted, what children do then to develop their activity themselves is crucial to the teacher in assessing what they have really learned and are able to use for other purposes and to other ends.

Any assessment can be summative or formative. Directed play has a formative approach in that the intervention is intended, following as it does from observation of the free play, to extend children's performance and learning and provide something from which they can move thinking forward. Summative assessment, on the other hand, would occur, for example, on completion of any product such as Beth's clay roof: she completed it successfully. Could the teacher have anticipated Beth's response to the new challenge of the roof. The answer is probably not, but she still needs to recognize the learning which has taken place.

Summative tests are usually those which give information on exactly what has been achieved to date, whereas diagnostic tests take a formative view of the child and suggest where additional learning opportunities need to be provided. Formal testing in play situations is unlikely, but as much of children's play has a product element (e.g. a model, a picture, a role enactment or a verbal story), teachers can, in fact, 'test' particular learning from the outcome. In doing this, the teacher or other adult will inevitably be prompted to consider further directed play. So the spiral will continue.

It is equally vital with young children to assess such traits as perseverance and concentration. Absorption in a task has been suggested by Armstrong as being most revealing about children and their course of learning. He feels that:

> these are the moments at which children are most in earnest, *however playfully*, and it is then ... that they reveal most about themselves, about the quality of their thought, about their own intellectual competence and about their capacity for sustained intellectual growth. (Armstrong, 1980:9; original emphasis)

Because much of assessment can be quite subjective, it is helpful at times for teachers to compare with others their individual assessments of children's activities. In fact, under the Task Group for Assessment and Testing (TGAT) proposals teachers will be asked to moderate other's assessments. This is no mean feat but aims to ensure that standards of assessment are consistent across schools and teachers. The activities shown in Fig. 7.7 and Table 7.5 attempt to give readers some flavour of a possible moderation exercise.

Children, surprisingly, are themselves frequently the best assessors and testers of what they have learned. Occasionally, they will quite exhaust

Fig. 7.7. Belinda's map of her route to school.

themselves in proving to themselves and others mastery over a particular activity or material. In assessing children's learning, discussions with the child as an individual can often produce the most useful information, especially as to concepts, knowledge and experiences gained which, when supported with observations and careful records, gives a good overall profile of that child. Even with those children who find difficulty for whatever reason in expressing what they know, adults are usually able to make assessments based on what they have produced or what processes they have been involved in (see Duncan and Dunn, 1988, for a fuller explanation of assessment and testing in the primary school).

Table 7.5. Rating Belinda's attempt at mapping.

Background information

After several activities on simple mapping, Belinda (together with other children in her group) was given the task of drawing a map to show her route to school. Figure 7.7 shows the results of her efforts

You must decide, alone in the first instance, given the following additional information, what rating you would give this attempt on a 0–5 scale

Additional information

Child's name – Belinda Smith
Age – 7 years, 7 months, top infant class
Happy at school, good concentration, works hard
Reading – test gave reading age of 8.6 years
Maths – test gave maths age of 7.5 years
Artistic ability deemed by teacher to be better than average as Belinda pays a
    good deal of attention to detail
Enjoys recording results of activities
One of those who live further away from the school

How do you rate Belinda? Circle at a point on the scale which you believe best fits this child's attempt at the task ...

    poor   0 : 1 : 2 : 3 : 4 : 5 :   very good

Now compare your result with another adult who has attempted the same activity. Any comments?

Finale

The role of the teacher is vital to children's effective communication and learning not because teachers necessarily teach didactically but because they provide the right structure and environment for effective play and learning to take place. Teachers will only know that this is occurring and that what is provided is appropriate if they are prepared to pay close attention to the observation, assessment and recording of the progress and development of individuals within their classes.

A warning note: there is a danger that we shall put adult interpretations on our observations and assessment of play. As Armstrong (1980:173) reminds us:

In the realm of play, of games, toys and make believe, children are already experts. The intellectual uses to which they put their expertise, in home, school, street and playground, reach out beyond the realm of childhood play, however, to embrace those adult traditions most commonly associated with classroom life, while, in turn, their early experience of literature, art or mathematics infiltrates both the form and content of their play.

Those children who, when readers have been considering the contents of this chapter, stand out for whatever reason as being different, are the subject of the next chapter.

8
Play and the 'Different' Child

The nature of individual needs is such that a single scenario is insufficient to capture the inevitable variety. Therefore, the following brief descriptions are of a small proportion of the children whose needs have evidenced themselves in the school context. Only the names of individual children have been changed, their essential characteristics being retained.

Matthew, aged 6 years, 6 months, was one of boy twins, a diabetic, whose mother was in her mid-40s at the time of the twins' arrival. For various reasons she resented the second born, Matthew. His individual needs were quite complex: he had little or no self-image, living permanently in his brother's shadow and, because of age, they were unfortunately assigned to the same class. Matthew constantly compared himself with his more outgoing and seemingly more intelligent twin. Matthew could not bring himself to play anything other than solitary games with small toys such as cars, any mildly physical play being quite out of the question for him, as far as he was concerned, in case he fell and went into glycoma shock.

Wayne arrived at school, just prior to his fifth birthday, determined to make his mark on the situation! On the very first morning, he dashed to an open shelf, dragged all the games, toys, jigsaws, interlocking cubes and other bits and pieces on to the floor, jumped on top of the lot and then hit another child over the head with the large, now empty, wooden Lego storage box. It transpired he had not been allowed toys at home as they were 'babyish' and his parents could not wait for him to grow up. For several weeks he caused havoc in the classroom with this uncontrollable and aggressive behaviour. Once, however, he established that playing with toys was fun and that if one damaged or maltreated them they would be removed (resulting, of course, in tantrums), he gradually toned down his wilder impulses. He remained very aggressive towards other children particularly in relation to the possession of toys.

Belinda, at 5 years, 5 months, had very retarded speech and her articulation was so poor that she might have been talking a foreign language! Discussions with her mother revealed a whole family of parents and three siblings whose speech was slow and poorly articulated, therefore providing the language model for this, the youngest child in the family. In play, she tried so hard to communicate with other children and they, in turn, listened, smiled and nodded but gave little in return. Her delight was to play in the home corner, dressed in the grandest clothes she could find, high heels and floppy brimmed hats, organizing the contents.

James, at 8 years, 2 months, was still so clumsy and physically awkward that it was necessary on one occasion to fetch the fire brigade to extract him from his classroom chair! He was a happy, cheerful boy, who made light of constantly falling over the smallest crack in the playground or the smallest step on his way into school. Needless to say, his recorded work was equally gross and untidy which served actually to hide a good deal of deep thought and creative ability. Even playing with constructional toys proved almost painful as James constantly struggled to fix pieces together. His delight, and the teacher's trauma, was to experiment in the water tray and he would 'invent' different carriers for water and different ways of letting the water out.

Lisa, at nearly 4, could carry on an adult conversation, read *The Times* and take nursery visitors on a conducted tour of the school grounds, naming every flower, tree, shrub, insect and weather pattern on the way. She proved to be exceptionally linguistically gifted with a good ear for sound and quickly learned to play several instruments almost self-taught. She delighted in fantasy play, using her highly active imagination to create breathtakingly sophisticated contexts for her own play and that of her friends.

Stephen, a child from a mixed-race background, who at the age of 6 called himself 'black', painted everything, however it started out, as dark brown or black and swore incessantly whenever frustrated. He would suddenly decide he had had enough of school and attempt a retreat to the local shops where he would inevitably steal sweets, chocolates or crisps. Stephen was competent in spoken language with an excellent vocabulary (sometimes of very choice words!) but his progress in academic learning was virtually non-existent. In physical play situations he excelled, being agile and capable.

Wendy, a bedraggled $3\frac{1}{2}$-year-old, sad-faced and red-eyed, would arrive at school with shoes just hanging on her feet, smelling rather potently. She loved sand and water play and painting straight and curved lines, but only if she was alone and if another child came near she would literally shrink away into a corner or under a table.

Jason, aged just over 7, frequently came to school black-eyed and limping. He found it difficult to look adults in the eye and always avoided contact. He would occasionally wet himself and be afraid to say until derided by another child. In play, he was very restless, moving from situation to situation as if he was afraid to stay still for even a minute. Concentration and persistence were very limited, with his longest attention span usually being given to the home corner teddy, who was Jason's frequent companion together with a selected peer friend. He was eventually put on the 'At Risk' Register, a victim of bullying and sexual harassment by his two older brothers with whom he shared a bedroom.

The majority of children come to nursery and main schools reasonably well-adjusted for their age and with few real problems except those of growing up in an ever-changing world. School is often the place where children find the most consistent adults, a secure environment for part of their day and plenty of playmates, play resources and materials through which to explore themselves in relation to other children, different adults and the environment outside the home. Yet, as suggested by the case studies cited above, there are some children whose needs identify them as different, as special in some way. The term 'special needs' (Warnock Report: DES, 1978), however, encompasses a wide range of mental and physical handicap and has connotations beyond the present intentions. The children identified above had different needs from those of a majority of their classmates *at the time of contact with them* and it is within this context that different needs rather than special needs will be considered.

Reflecting on individual needs will necessitate looking at problems and difficulties but it is vital that we do not 'label' children. Hargreaves (1975:39) warns strongly of the dangers by saying that 'once the teacher has categorized a pupil he is likely to resist having to recategorize' but categorization has the 'potentiality for stimulating a self-fulfilling prophecy'. Teachers must constantly review by careful and objective observations their impressions of individuals and recognize when change has occurred. Children's individual needs only become a major problem when they present difficulties and obstacles to other children's learning, enjoyment, concentration, and so on. For example, Matthew, Lisa and Wendy caused no difficulties for their classmates, Stephen tended to be hero-worshipped and really only Wayne produced any problems for his peers.

Teachers must inevitably deal with individual needs in the context of the larger social setting of the classroom and this creates enormous challenges and dilemmas, but as Brierley (1987:108) suggests: 'it is just to treat different persons differently so long as each is treated as well as possible'. As one of the major functions of both school and play is that of socialization, it is natural and effective that they should occur together.

The children cited above varied in their ability to undertake social play: what is consistent is that each child found some way through play of both expressing and normally satisfying their individual need to some degree. What is even more important is that the teacher was able to use each child's play interest to promote the establishment of a greater self-concept, confidence in attempting new activities and enabled the furtherance of that individual's learning. Many of these children if forced into formal learning situations would have quickly established themselves as disaffected individuals with whom interaction might prove a constant battle. For as Clark (1988:276) has established through her lengthy and thorough research:

> already by five years of age there are very wide differences in the readiness of children for more formal aspects of education and their grasp of the underlying concepts on which to build numeracy and literacy.

Looking to a child's strengths serves incidentally to help the teacher. There is always the danger that a child fails to learn by a particular teacher's standards, which makes the teacher feel a failure (Clifford, 1983:282), and this, of course, must be avoided at all costs.

Play in itself can serve both to identify children's individual needs and provide palliative measures. A child who constantly reprimands the home corner inhabitants for wetting the bed, could indicate a fairly obvious personal situation past or present and a chat with the parent could well clarify this and enable all minds to be put at ease. Other situations are not so straightforward and a speedy and basic interpretation may be misleading and harmful. Particular instances such as child abuse of some form would be a prime example, as in Jason's case above. It would, for example, be easy to conclude from seeing a child seriously maltreating a doll, that the child too had been beaten. This may be so, but equally the child could be trying out something he had witnessed on television or because of his own inner frustrations. It is important not to jump to conclusions, but it is equally important that children who express individual needs in whatever form have their play monitored to see whether they are isolated incidents or something more serious.

Play can also prevent some children's difficulties from occurring, as in the case of the child who plays out a situation which causes them concern (e.g. the death of a grandparent) until understanding and comfort are established. Play can indeed provide therapy for the temporarily disturbed, perturbed or handicapped child (Musselwhite, 1986), though not enough recent research has been undertaken about play and its effects on longer-term disturbance to provide any conclusive evidence. Children who cannot play, such as Wayne, are 'poorer' for the lack of such ability

and it does appear that those children who can play derive enormous benefit from it (Rutter, 1982).

There is no doubt at all that for a vast majority of children play is a real
motivator – it has its own intrinsic rewards, it is done spontaneously and
voluntarily and it is thoroughly enjoyable (Bronfenbrenner, 1979). Those
children reluctant to engage in school 'work' will almost inevitably engage
in school 'play' and teachers must ensure that they direct that play in
order that both situations provide the same 'end-product' of learning. As
Dawson (1985:4) suggests, the long-term effects of meeting and responding to individual needs will be worth the effort in preventing the 'entrench-
ment or exacerbation of special needs'.

The caring role of adults sometimes conflicts with control. Children
must know that whatever they do we still care for them, although we
equally disapprove of unwelcome behaviour. We must value the child
despite his or her faults and failings – even teachers have them! Children
who do have difficulties often have more than one: for example, difficulties
in socialization often lead to aggressive behaviour towards other children;
learning problems can lead to behaviour problems and vice versa. These
children in particular need our understanding and affection if they are to
thrive. Similarly, it is vital that we identify, analyse, interpret and handle

Plate 11. Play has its own intrinsic rewards, it is done spontaneously and
voluntarily and it is thoroughly enjoyable.

		1	2	3**
Developmental	Speech retardation*			
	Perception			
	Coordination: fine/gross motor			
	Lack of self-control			
	General immaturity			
	Over-active/restless			
	Wetter or soiler			
Behavioural	Aggression			
	Bullying			
	Moodiness/being uncooperative			
	Distractive			
	Disruptive/fidgety			
	Disobedient			
	Attention-seeking			
	Swearing			
	Stealing			
	Quiet/solitary			
Learning	Concentration/short attention span			
	Persistence			
	Poor retention and memory			
	Specific: language/speech			
	reading			
	mathematics/science			
	Lack of general experiences			
	English as a second language			
	Poor or lack of imagination			
Socialization	Separation difficulties/school refusal			
	Dependency			
	Solitary/lonely			
	Lack of confidence with other			
	children/adults			
	Over-confidence			
	Self-contained and self-sufficient			
Emotional	Unhappiness/tears			
	Fears/anxieties/worries/nail-biting			
	Lack of confidence in self			
	Sadness			
	Anger/frustration/lies			
	Need for love and respect			
	Abused children			
	Over-particular/fussy			
Health needs	Asthma			
	Eczema			
	Diabetes			
	Epilepsy/fits			
	Lack of sleep/fresh air			
	Overweight/underweight			

Fig. 8.1.

Key to Fig. 8.1. Some commonly found individual needs in 4- to 8-year-olds.
*Each of these areas is open to ready extension/expansion by adults.
**It is possible to modify this list as a checklist for individual children, in which case it would need the addition of Name and Date of birth. This third column would be marked 1, 2 or 3, dependent upon the needs of the particular child: 1 = no real problem; 2 = some indications of need in this area; 3 = need certainly evident. The outcome of making such a rating is self-evident.

---

individual needs as early a possible to minimize the effects upon the child of constantly failing, misbehaving, being unhappy or lacking friends and confidence.

The children whose individual needs were outlined at the beginning of this chapter, share with many others a number of problems, difficulties and needs which are common in many schools. A few others are also worth identification. Figure 8.1 outlines the most common individual needs that I have encountered and Table 8.1 itemizes a few play situations in which these needs have frequently been met successfully. Some further expansion seems necessary in terms of the identified individual needs, and some strategies and approaches for dealing with them.

Table 8.1. Play situations for meeting some individual needs.

General play activities, with a variety of materials and resources readily available in normal classrooms, will significantly help every child both in the identification and satisfaction of individual needs. A majority of play resources develop features such as confidence, imagination and the opportunity to socialize. Frequently lacking the words they need to express feelings, the youngest children will often exhibit these through their play. Specific needs can certainly be met to some extent by specific play situations, some of which are indicated below

Play cannot solve all identified needs or problems, for example, the child who swears will need certain handling throughout all his activities and particularly at times when the unwanted behaviour is apparent. As swearing frequently occurs through attention-seeking behaviour the obvious treatment (ignoring it) can be undertaken in all situations

Table 8.1 continued

Material/activity	Examples of play potential
Clay, dough, woodwork, sand, water, large blocks	Aggressive and disruptive children can have satisfaction in being legitimately constructive and destructive. They allow sociability: although children frequently work alone with these materials, they at least ensure that children work in parallel or even cooperatively with peers
Mini-worlds play	Bossy children and bullies often gain great satisfaction in controlling their own mini-world of garage, farm or doll's house. Acquisitive children can make small junk items for this play and be allowed to retain them. Imagination has the chance to grow from the real and current experiences of the child in the realm of fantasy and future
Puppets, telephones, open-fronted TV, mirrors	All ideal for the child with language needs of any kind. Two telephones (or home-made ones) will encourage interaction. A television (without tube) or a large cardboard box with a screen cut-out, will encourage budding newsreaders and weather forecasters who, if supplied with dressing-up clothes, will also dress for the occasion! Children with articulation difficulties are often helped greatly by play in front of a mirror, particularly if they have an adult model for their words and sounds
Sorting – natural and man-made materials	The obvious choice for children with perceptual difficulties and for those with retention problems
Teacher-made and commercial, card and board games, and derivations, Kim's game and pelmanism	These greatly aid motivation and concentration and can help children gain self-control, particularly if, in the early days, they are played with an accompanying adult. The latter two particularly aid memory, as do talking games like 'I went to the baker and I bought ...', participants having to remember objects in sequence
Teddies, dolls, action man, play-people	Soft toys in particular can help the lonely or distressed child in giving comfort and companionship. These materials can help the child work through a problem at second-hand in the

Material/activity	Examples of play potential
	same way as books and stories but with the child being basically in control
Large indoor and outdoor apparatus and locomotor resources	These can often give the tired or lethargic child (or the over-active child) a chance to gain some feelings of physical and mental well-being
Individual and group discussion with an adult	Of value in satisfying just about the whole range of needs likely to be met with young children, but need careful consideration if the children themselves are genuinely going to do most of the talking. It is through such activities also that children who normally command little respect can be given an attentive audience and personal esteem
Excursions, outside school, listening walks, visits, etc.	Obvious for those children who lack general experiences, find communication difficult, or have perceptual needs. Those lacking self-control are frequently helped by being given responsibility for themselves and their possessions
Shops, home corner, dressing up	Probably the one activity which satisfies a majority of needs if set-up adequately, appropriately and with variety to attract different ages, sexes, cultures. Younger children can sort out the 'I, you, they' confusions, learn cooperation, coordination of own and others' needs, use language, imagination, patience, experience and concentration. The shy or abused child can 'be' someone else for a short while, the lonely child can have companionship. The child on medication can be the doctor and give others pretend doses: the list is endless

Finally – and very obviously:

Picture books	Language development, repetition of familiar words and sound patterns, group identity and individuality are all catered for in books. The lonely child will be encouraged to be part of the group, children lacking experiences will benefit, as may those who suffer fears and anxieties about themselves and their own lives.

Developmental needs

Delay in learning often occurs in schools where a child is particularly immature or is clumsy, like James described at the start of this chapter. Immaturity covers all developmental domains – cognitive, social, emotional, moral and physical – and is relatively easily identifiable using the basic developmental checklists and guidelines suggested in Chapter 7. Immature children are prime candidates for carefully conceived play activities, through which basic conceptual understandings can be achieved and, for James, coordination, manipulation and physical control can be encouraged. Some children mature fairly rapidly and any problems associated with immaturity have no time to become ingrained. Those who are generally slow to mature can only do so in their own time and often require a great deal of variety and stimulation to promote even very small steps in basic learning.

Individual differences in development frequently become obvious only when a child joins a group of others of similar age and normal spread of abilities and maturity levels. Even then the children can be going through 'transitions' which result in the child 'coming unglued' for a time (Bee and Mitchell, 1988:75), while physical emotional and intellectual changes compete within the developmental system. Developmental delay, on the other hand, can be due to the child's innate characteristics, but occasionally can be due to the individual wishing to remain a child for a variety of reasons often associated with over-protective parents. Matthew, the twin described above, rejected by his mother, also had to withstand her over-protectiveness toward his brother, which developed into a self-initiated shield for Matthew supported by his diabetes.

We must accept that, while development is incremental in certain ways (a child cannot run before walking, talk before babbling), it is also regressive: all children revert occasionally to play situations which one might expect they would have outgrown and this, in itself, can sometimes signify a current trauma. The spiral nature of learning through play, rather than the linear structure often associated with curriculum areas such as mathematics, allows for this and teachers must accept that such regression is natural for some children in certain contexts. Children are frequently seen to revert for a short time when re-starting school in a new class.

Behavioural needs

This category of needs appears to create by far and above the most problems for teachers. In a large class, behaviourally deviant children sap the adults' energies, fray tempers and occasionally result in emotions becoming out of all proportion to the situation – from both sides. They present problems for peers in that aggressive children, for example, have been shown to engage in little individual play, preferring to play in groups which they then totally dominate verbally and physically (Manning and Herrmann, 1988). There often seems to be no outward reason why this aggressive behaviour should occur. Wayne's behavioural difficulties were fairly easily discovered in discussion with his parents and they proved also to be his eventual salvation, with a little help from the school. Wayne, his mother and the teacher had several sessions after school when he played with a variety of materials and mother and teacher discussed all the things he was learning. After more than 6 months, the parents began to realize that the child needed to be allowed freedom to grow, talk and develop and playthings, which had been borrowed from the school in the earlier stages, were discussed with the teacher and finally bought for the child. Almost overnight he became an easier child to handle, if not a model pupil! His aggressive behaviour to other children, however, took longer to remedy. Isolating a child with behaviour problems is always a major decision. However, it was agreed with Wayne that an area of the classroom was his. This helped his self-identity and he was able to hoard his collection (bottle tops, cubes, other children's lunches, toy cars and a myriad of other things) without too much concern to other children. The breakthrough came nearly a year later when he invited another child to view his collection.

It does seem from personal experience and research (see Smith and Green, 1975) that boys have a greater probability of being involved in aggressive incidents than girls and adult intervention is necessary if the dominated child is likely to come to harm. There are occasions, however, when some minor acts of aggression are best ignored or de-escalated by facial expression or body language rather than negatively reinforced.

Deviant behaviour of any kind must be the concern of everyone in the school as well as the child's parents. Any attempts to modify behaviour must be consistent throughout the child's waking life. Any rewards, however minimal, should also be consistent. Children are shrewd manipulators, particularly of caring adults, and this must be avoided at all costs. So adults must decide:

1. What exactly needs to be changed – not simply 'aggressive behaviour' but specific actions. List them and then prioritize the list (no attempt should be made to work on too many changes at once).
2. Assess frequency by observation (see below) and accumulate a record of occurrences.
3. Decide what is to be ignored and what is to be encouraged. Think carefully about the context and the particular child.
4. Consider ways in which acceptable behaviour can be rewarded, such as *extra* play with favoured materials, playing with the child, praising and verbal encouragement.

5. Share the decision making among all those concerned and agree to operate a common policy of rewards.

It must always be remembered that through aggressive, destructive or intimidating play, children are often portraying personal problems just as Wayne did. Nothing will be gained by nagging the child or constantly complaining about the behaviour, but everything can be gained both for child and teacher by accepting that children have feelings for which they need an outlet. The child needs to be provided with a more acceptable outlet such as gross physical play, constructive and destructive play or role play. Aggression is not a bad thing in itself: some aggression serves essential biological functioning and makes people strive to try a little harder. Rough-and-tumble bouts in children's play have also been shown to unite the players and encourage socialization rather than the reverse (Cohen, 1987).

In considering behaviour, it is vital that we remember the overly quiet, introverted or withdrawn child whose behaviour does not demand attention in the same way as the aggressive child, but whose needs are frequently equal if not greater. This type of child either plays alone or in parallel with other children but rarely if ever becomes one of a group. Belinda, described earlier in the chapter, would gradually become just such a child without the teacher's sensitivity and appropriate intervention. Many of these types of children are the ones the teacher cannot even remember having contact with during the day: this is easily remedied by the use of a tally system alongside a duplicated class list which will quickly inform the teacher as to which children have had contact and how often during any particular day or week.

Learning needs

The ability of children to learn and their speed of learning differ. Similarly, they can show skill and motivation in some areas of learning and not in others. Personal experience suggests that a majority of children's learning difficulties stem from language-related problems and the wealth of material and resources available for remediation of a whole range of language skills lends support to this view. Bee (1985), rightly, uses this fact to support the very close links between language and cognition. Class matrices, as described in Chapter 7, will quickly show which children are not achieving at the level of the majority and, if such matrices are kept for several different purposes, such as skill development and curriculum areas, where the learning needs occur will be quickly identified.

Play has been shown by several researchers, among them Irwin and Frank, to facilitate the acquisition of speech and language skills because

'In the course of their play children argue, discuss, explore, plot and talk together' (Irwin and Frank, 1981:222). A group of students and I undertook a small study of free and directed play and found that richer and more varied verbal communication occurred between peers, particularly in pairs (thus supporting once again the work of Sylva *et al.*, 1980) in free play activity compared with directed activity. However, during directed activities the children increased their vocabulary and conceptual knowledge which became evident during subsequent free play. Children were also motivated to talk and discuss their actions when an adult became a parallel player. Where students played with a material or activity themselves, the children appeared to take a greater interest and achieved more in terms of communication, motivation and general learning.

In addition to language, perceptual difficulties sometimes cause children to exhibit individual needs in relation to classification and categorization, and play situations tend to provide a fairly rapid evaluation of a child's ability to sort materials, discuss colours and shapes, discriminate between textures or put parts together to create a whole.

Socialization and individual needs

Its quality of providing a means and purpose for socialization is often the greatest claim made for play opportunities by teachers and, indeed, some play situations lend themselves well to this purpose, e.g. pretend play in the shop or home corner or cooperative play in the construction of a roadway for vehicles. But play can often lead to children being quite solitary (Sutton-Smith, 1986) as they involve themselves in achieving certain self-regulated goals or work at representing something in painting. Much of what is provided in the majority of classrooms encourages parallel rather than cooperative, social play and, in this context, directed play can encourage social play by setting children cooperative tasks. Inevitably, the youngest children will spend longer periods perhaps in parallel play while they learn what socializing with others is all about. According to Chazan and Laing (1982:54) 'social maturity includes evolving a style of coping with frustration as well as learning how to share and join in'.

Periods of solitary play need not cause concern: we all need time to ourselves and children are no different. Erikson (1950:194) explains a child's need for solitary play by saying that it 'remains an indispensable harbor for the overhauling of shattered emotions after periods of rough going in the social seas'. Our concern must be with the child who regularly plays alone or is constantly peripheral to other children's play activities. Even in these situations, however, there is some evidence that children who prefer solitary activities concentrate for longer periods, are more persistent and more highly creative and imaginative (Strom, 1981b:47). Strom goes so far as to say that every child's experience should 'include a generous period of time for solitary play' (Strom, 1981b:50). Perhaps a deeper concern should be for the child who appears not to be able to play at all but, thankfully, this is rare, though occasionally children from different ethnic backgrounds need encouragement to play (see below). Traumatic events can sometimes inhibit a child's play for some time and the child's attitude and ability to play is impeded while the mental problem is worked through (Webb, 1967:51). In these circumstances teachers can only watch, wait and be sympathetic and supportive of the individual and allow the child a choice of activities until the problem is resolved. Ballard and Crooks (1985) report that low levels of social peer involvement among kindergarten children could be substantially increased by showing them a video of children playing happily together and then discussing with the children friendships and playmates. Perhaps this indicates the need for some children to observe others at play as encouragement to participate.

Most children who are initially reluctant to play at nursery gradually become players through a process of spectating, peripheral play and parallel play before engaging fully in social play, and this can take some time. It is beholden of teachers to know at what stage in play each of the children in their care is at any one time, and observation will again enable decisions to be made as to which children frequently play alone, in pairs, cooperatively. In this regard, the teacher should also monitor children's play in the variety of situations already described in Table 1.1. The use of a simple matrix will at least show which types of play are regularly engaged in, by which children, and whether a balance between individual and social play is achieved.

A child who comes to school fearful of losing a parent will not be able to play effectively or cooperatively until he or she has confidence in the situation and the new adults. This is best achieved by either persuading the parent to stay for some time to settle the child down or attaching a member of staff or volunteer to the particular child for the first part of the session.

Health needs

Children at different times come to school tired, about to develop a childhood illness, or feeling generally out-of-sorts, and teachers are quick to spot the signs and take effective action. There are still children, like Jason, whose tiredness is ingrained in some greater problem and children who regularly fall asleep at school need to be noted. Some schools recognize that many of the children will not have been adequately fed before starting out for school and ensure that a snack and a drink are provided fairly early on in the morning. Hungry and tired children can rarely play or learn effectively and certainly can rarely undertake the gross physical play which promotes a feeling of general well-being and eagerness to pursue the next activity. Wetton (1988:34) emphasizes that 'Children who are physically healthy are more able to function properly in intellectual and social interchange', yet suggests that there is growing evidence of incipient heart disease among young children due mostly to sedentary life-styles. Physical play in schools is probably the least well-provided for, certainly in terms of developing quality and body control, and many children have a real need for thorough physical exertion with vigorous large motor movements designed to increase strength and power and promote growth. Many girls in particular appear to engage very infrequently in physical play, except that directed during apparatus or movement sessions by the teacher. Wetton's (1983) studies give some evidence that 4-year-olds were no longer being challenged by the physical play provided and this was one of the main reasons for them avoiding or disregarding such activity.

In relation to health education, young children's sexuality occasionally becomes evident in some play situations and exploration of genitals is not uncommon, particularly during 'hospital' pretend play. This is quite

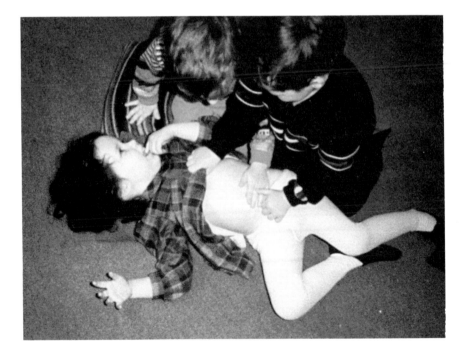

Plate 12. Young children's sexuality occasionally becomes evident in some play situations, particularly during 'hospital' pretend play.

normal, particularly among children whose siblings are of the same sex and who begin to realize sex differences. However, if this becomes an obsession and permeates play over a longer period, an explanation should be sought. In the case of a child who blackmailed others into exposing themselves before he would let them go to the toilet, it was discovered that he frequently watched pornographic videos in the evening with his father while his mother was out at work and he was trying to come to terms with what he saw.

Cultural needs

Having another language is decidedly an advantage rather than a problem but, as most schools are still basically oriented to the English language, children whose mother tongue is other than English will have specific needs if their own language is to be maintained and developed and competence in the use of English is also to be acquired.

Different cultures value play differently, some not at all. Moving from a home where play may well not have a place within the cultural value system to a classroom whose basic emphasis is on learning through play, can create significant conflicts for young children. Some children from different ethnic backgrounds request 'work' and attitudes take a long time to change, particularly if that change remains unsupported within the home environment. A policy of discussing classroom activities as 'working with the sand' or 'working with the bricks' is a step in the right direction, and discussing with the child what has been learned through these activities is a useful strategy. Similarly, directing children's play and offering a 'work' challenge can increase motivation to play, as can pairing an unwilling player with another child who thrives on challenging play activities.

Abused children and their needs

Evidence of abuse, be it physical, emotional or sexual is tenuous at the best of times as the Cleveland Enquiry (1988) revealed. Abused children like Jason have somehow an appearance of maturity beyond their years yet, at the same time, seem to scream out to be children. Teachers will usually have all the necessary information regarding children considered to be at risk and will want to monitor the child's general appearance, demeanour and attitudes regularly. It is advisable, particularly if outside agencies are already or are likely to be involved, to keep a special notebook on a suspected abuse victim, noting anything unusual or of concern whenever necessary with dates and factual descriptions.

Sexually abused children, it has been shown by Madge Bray (Cohen, 1988), are significantly helped to come to terms with assault by playing with anatomically correct dolls, telephones, puppets, and so on, with a child therapist and exploring what has happened to them. This is far too specialist for the classroom teacher and indeed it would be a dangerous tactic to attempt without proper training, but watching and listening to the child at play alone and with peers can give indications of abuse situations and confirm the necessity for action. Maher (1987) believes that teachers must play a continuing and major role in identifying child-abuse victims and be trained in all necessary skills. Obvious indicators of abuse such as bruising can often occur to children in normal play activities – climbing trees, riding bicycles – but other signs are manifested, such as the inability to play, frequently wetting and soiling, withdrawal, abnormal fears, unexplained absences and, occasionally, masturbation. Stern (1987:44) suggests that one of the main indictors of abuse in schoolchildren is a slow and gradual behavioural change which teachers are in the best position, if sensitive to such changes, to identify.

Self-concept and emotional needs

Any kinds of difficulties and problems may result in a child having a poor self-image and low self-esteem, and their ability to learn, make friends or behave appropriately will be jeopardized. A poor self-concept can also be a result of a child not yet having established itself as a unique individual. As Herron and Sutton-Smith (1982:10) suggest: 'To establish a separate identity ... the child must literally get outside himself and apprehend himself from some other perspective.' Role play provides a prime vehicle for this to occur and teachers need, through their resource provision, to ensure that role play opportunities are made available and inspire the whole range of interests of the class. Specific individual needs can be met, e.g. responsibility for being the shopkeeper can be given to children who rarely feel adequate to undertake such responsibility.

Children with low self-esteem tend to give up easily before they have developed the 'depth of knowledge ... central to the child's development' (Bruce, 1987). Yet the sheer motivation of play situations generally means that concentration will be given to activities if they are appropriate for the child's needs and if they provide success and praise for succeeding.

Gender differences can also create poor self-images or feelings of inadequacy in certain areas. For years girls have been implicitly told they are less mathematically able than boys and they have tended to live up to this. There is some evidence of girls having innately less well-developed spatial abilities than boys (MacDonald, 1985) but the majority of differences are created environmentally. Brierley (1987:63) believes that 'numerical, experimental and spatial activities should be stage managed for girls', and this must apply to directed play for girls' individual needs as well as providing and promoting situations in which boys can exhibit care, patience and gentleness. Singer and Singer (1981) feel that this will not occur unless more male teachers enter early childhood education, while The Equal Opportunities Commission in an undated pamphlet, *Equal Start*, feel that adult expectations have the most significant influence (p. 14).

Without a concept of self there is no self-discipline, self-control, or knowledge of others and your affect on them. A shaky self-image can be bolstered with a great deal of praise at every suitably praiseworthy event, applause from the other children for good results, and the like. An almost non-existent or damaged self-image, as in the case of Stephen, can defeat even the best teacher and probably requires psychological help beyond the scope of the normal class teacher. Stephen was able to overcome some of his problems through using his remarkable physical capabilities as a starting point for praise and encouragement. He initiated movement sequences for others to emulate, made huge climbing structures and set other children physical challenges, but still, when the chips were down, accused everyone of getting at him for being black.

Lack of self-image can be created by inconsistent handling in the child's background, personality, lack of opportunity to gauge self against peers and lack of occasion to explore one's own feelings and emtions. Role play, mini-worlds play, physical play and discussion about activities and feelings towards them with a caring adult as well as other children will help most children to develop more self-confidence and self-esteem.

Identifying needs through observation

In Chapter 7 the importance of observation was emphasized and this is nowhere more vital than in understanding individual needs and developing remediating tactics. Behavioural needs, in particular, often seem to dominate a classroom and one purpose of close observation is to put such incidents into perspective. A child can seem to be constantly hitting other children or throwing things around, yet a closer inspection will reveal that this actually occurs quite infrequently and that it is the prolonged consequences of the action which create the impression of greater frequency. Figures 8.2 and 8.3 cover identification and observation respectively and can be developed so that consideration can be given to all the specific needs identified above.

It is tempting to think that a majority of problems and individual needs stem from the child's home background and to see the school as a panacea. However, we are not entirely blameless! We sometimes create our own problems by the way the day or the classroom is organized. We all know of the child who is terrified to enter the playground, the child who hates going into assembly with the crowd, or the one who bursts into tears when dinner time arrives. We must strive, however difficult this is within the normal organization, to allow these children time to resolve their fears.

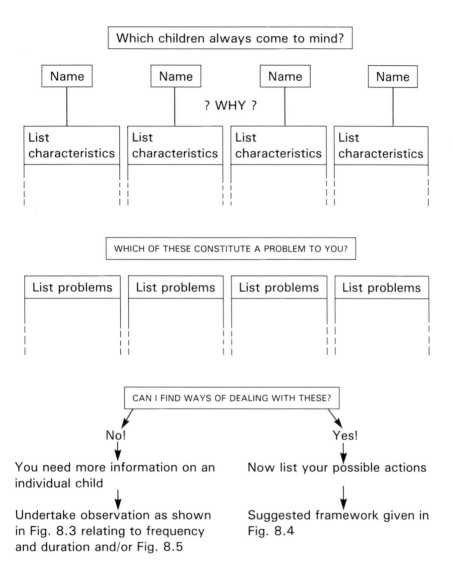

Fig. 8.2. Identifying children causing concern.

Classrooms which are organized around group tables do not take into account the needs of the child who is easily distracted by being able to see the faces and activities of at least six peers. Small individual or pair bays around the walls of the classroom can do much to give these children security and the opportunity to develop concentration. Physical space is worthy of lengthy consideration, particularly in the light of the research of Smith and Connolly (1977) who discovered that lack of physical space increased aggressive behaviour among young children.

Child's name .... Date of birth ....

Any special features/notes regarding this child ....

....

Length of time you have been concerned ....

Trait/characteristic/behaviour/learning observed ....

....

Observations made for session/half-day/whole day/*x* days/1 week
(decide on frequency)

Date	Time	Duration	Stimulus (what was the prompt?)	Outcome	Others involved

Add notes on:

When was child behaving/working/playing *appropriately*?

With whom?

With what?

Did incidents recorded above cause child distress/concern?

Did you intervene?   When?   Why?

How did child respond to the intervention?

Fig. 8.3. Observation of the needs of one child.

Taking children out of their normal environment and away from their normal teacher for special treatment of any kind rarely solves the child's or the teacher's problem in the long term. If extra teaching help is available, it is better used to relieve the teacher of the rest of her class in order for her to give concentration to the needs of individuals. In this way the adult who knows the children best can deal with them in the context of current topics and in the way the class normally operates, thus ensuring that normal routines, so vital to children with any kind of problem, remain unaltered.

A few further points in planning to meet individual needs

First, we must establish the child successfully in his or her play, even if this means allowing the exploration of a particular material over and over again. At this stage there is no intention of directing the play unless the child shows every sign of inviting this. However, the adult should, whenever possible, be present, not only to support the play but also to observe and monitor changes in the child's attitudes or abilities.

All children with individual needs have some strengths or particular interests or talents which can form the starting point for attempting to alleviate their difficulties or promote learning. We must always begin from where the child can succeed and gain enjoyment. This is more often than not in play experiences.

Some individual needs, such as those of the abused child, are outside the scope of teachers to deal with, and it will be necessary to call in outside agencies after appropriate consulation with parents.

Aggressive children need an outlet and their needs can often be satisfied by the inclusion within the day's programme of activities using clay, sand, water, woodwork, large apparatus work and/or large constructional toys.

Concluding remarks

Nowadays, the teaching profession is more sensitive and sophisticated in responding to individual children's needs. We tend to look more realistically at children and the factors which create difficulties. One feature of modern life for a majority of adults is stress, perhaps particularly in the teaching profession itself! Modern forms of stress are just as likely to affect children, in all situations, including family and school, and much of what we perceive as apparent psychological difficulties may well be stress-related. It is important that we ensure stress is kept to a minimum in our own classroom. If there appears to be an inordinate amount of a particular difficulty (e.g. behaviour problem), one should ask oneself 'What is it really like to be in my class? Would I like to be one of the children? Do I create or diminish anxiety for them? Would I find the activities interesting, stimulating and would I want to be here?' We must not credit children with anything we do not feel ourselves: if our response to our own classroom situation is a relatively negative one, then why should the children feel any different?

We are all aware of those children who are always so evident in the answers to the questions should build up as complete a picture of the needs presented by the identified child and outline possible ways of dealing with them

Name .... Date of birth ....

Specify individual areas which most urgently require your attention

1.   2.   3.   ...

Detail any techniques/strategies/materials/activities which you have at any time found successful in helping the child

1.   2.   3.   ...

Give (if possible) examples of positive things the child is able to do in the area(s) selected. (Starting from what the child can do is vital!)

1.   2.   3.   ...

List as many play activities as possible which the child seems to enjoy and which could promote satisfaction of the presently identified needs

1.   2.   3.   ...

List any situations/activities which particularly seems to lead to the child making:

(A)   Positive responses

(B)   Negative responses

From your observations, write down any activity/situation/adult/other child whom the child seems particularly at odds or unhappy with

1.   2.   3.   ...

Fig. 8.4. Dealing with identified needs.

classroom situation, the ones the visitors always seem to talk to and look to for a response. Which children always come to mind for you? The activity already suggested in Fig. 8.3 might help to rationalize thinking about those children who really have different needs and those who are just very evident characters but otherwise quite normal! Figures 8.3–8.6 provide a suggested framework which teachers may apply to both short- and longer-term planning for the needs of individual children.

In school work it has been shown that children generally achieve at a much lower level than their ability suggests (Brennan, 1979). Yet, in play, according to Vygotsky (1978:102): 'the child always behaves beyond his

Name of Child .... Date of Birth ....

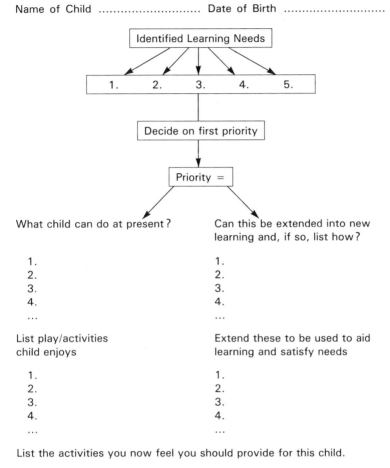

What child can do at present?

1.
2.
3.
4.
...

List play/activities
child enjoys

1.
2.
3.
4.
...

Can this be extended into new
learning and, if so, list how?

1.
2.
3.
4.
...

Extend these to be used to aid
learning and satisfy needs

1.
2.
3.
4.
...

List the activities you now feel you should provide for this child.

1.
2.
3.
4.
...
...

Are the appropriate resources (materials/personnel) available? Make
plans to obtain as necessary.

Do any other children need similar activities? Make plans to group
accordingly.

Will my classroom organization need modification? Make plans to
modify accordingly.

Fig. 8.5. Charting learning needs.

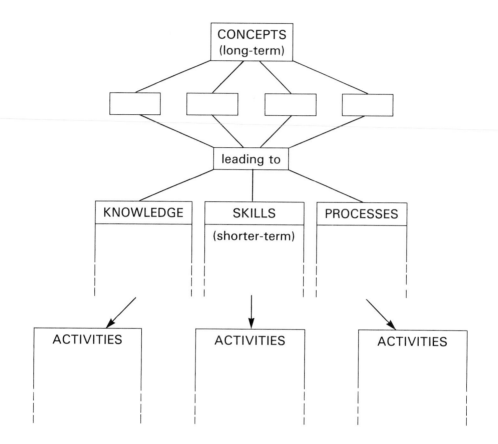

Fig. 8.6. Planning for longer-term learning. These plans can be for individuals, groups or whole-class teaching. It is suggested that, if used for individual children, teachers should use colour-code insertions to show where children already have skills, are part-way to developing them or have as yet no experience or abilities.

average age, above his daily behaviour. In play, it is as if he were a head taller than himself.' It is absolutely vital that teachers totally accept and remember this through all the pressures that are inevitably brought upon them to push children into formal learning.

Working with children who have individual and different needs is very time-consuming, but then so is dealing with the problems that arise by *not* doing so. Teachers can spend an inordinate amount of time simply dealing with problems as they occur and must decide whether this time would not be better spent analysing *why* it is occurring and making efforts to reduce it to everyone's advantage.

Contact with parents of children with specific needs is a must, as only they can supply information about the child in contexts other than the school. Their knowledge of their own child is inevitably superior in many respects and they can only support the staff's efforts to help that child towards greater learning if they themselves are put in the picture and made sympathetic to your aims. Many parents simply do not understand what play activities can provide for their children and it is vital that teachers are able to explain why some children appear to be spending a great deal of their day at play. The next chapter explores relationships with parents and possible ways of exploring play and learning expectations with them.

9

Play and Adult Expectations

Three hypothetical, though reality-based incidents, will serve to highlight some of the issues worthy of attention, particularly in relation to the sometimes conflicting expectations of teachers and parents in relation to children's play activities.

In this first instance, the viewpoint is that of the parent:

Jane, aged 6, has come home from school covered in glue, the kind that is nigh impossible to remove. You have received a note of apology from the teacher (though not an explanation!) which says the head has also been informed. The next morning, you decide to go to school intent on telling the teacher just what you think of her 'practical curriculum'. All the children in the class are busy with what looks like a confusing mass of activities when you go in. You get very frustrated trying to tell the teacher your grievances over all this mess and noise. You begin to feel even more annoyed – don't they ever do any proper, quiet work in this class?

In the second example, the viewpoint is that of the teacher:

Yesterday, the parent who regularly helps you in the classroom started some knitting with a group of children. The class have been working on a topic about 'Our Village' and, from an idea you saw at a local art exhibition, the idea of knitting squares and possibly triangles to form basic house shapes for a collage, appealed to you and the children. Knitting is also a new experience for many of the children and the kind of manual dexterity, hand–eye coordination and manipulation skills, plus another perspective on the shapes that is involved will challenge some of your 7-year-olds. The children are keen and interested, particularly Graham, a usually rather dour boy, with few interests except mathematics and football. Graham gets very involved in his knitting project and, surprisingly, masters the skills quite quickly. He pleads to take his knitting home and you are only too pleased that he is so interested. The next morning, however, you've hardly arrived in school before a very red-faced, irate father thrusts the knitting at you saying: 'How dare you turn my boy into a cissy! Don't you ever let him do anything like this again!' All this occurs in front of the child who looks near to tears. Without waiting for an explanation the parent leaves.

Even the youngest children are not too young to have a point of view, as the third example indicates:

> You are Peter and $5\frac{1}{2}$ years old. You do some quite good writing which the teacher has directed you to do and which you found quite easy. She gives you a gold star on your page and you show your friend Jonathan. Then you work really hard with some sums but somehow you just can't get it all together. Then suddenly you think you've got the idea. You write down all the answers, take your book to the teacher and she puts crosses all over the page. No gold star! Later that day you do a painting which the teacher praises really highly: all the other children think it's fantastic. You feel very proud. Can you have a gold star you ask. The teacher laughs and tells you that gold stars are only for good work.

Of major importance in these incidents is that each person involved appears to be taking little account of the feelings, understandings and values of the others. Yet this empathy for others is a vital prerequisite to children's learning. If home and school are in conflict about play situations (or any other 'issues') it is hardly to be expected that the child will be open to the learning processes in either situation. What makes any lack of shared values and expectations more difficult to understand is that many teachers are themselves parents, and a reasonable expectation would be that appreciation of parental viewpoints would be simpler for them than in the obverse situation, where fewer parents are themselves teachers. Each of the adult parties needs equally to consider the albeit inexperienced viewpoint of the child as shown in the third incident above. Despite the teacher clearly having an established reward system which she understands, this had not been portrayed effectively to the child and, in any case, the suitability of a reward system which so clearly distinguishes work and play would be highly questionable to those who agree with the present stance.

Different perceptions

It is helpful to reflect on the instances above from the three different viewpoints of parent, teacher or child. For example, the teacher in the first scene might feel aggrieved because, despite her concern about the extent of glue on the child's clothing, informing the head and writing a letter of apology to the parent, she still had to deal with the complaining parent right at the start of the school day when really she was more concerned to ensure that the children were all purposefully occupied. She might question why this parent appears not to realize that the teacher has more than her problems to contend with first thing in the morning! And, in any case, children should not be sent to school in good clothing; parents must expect school to be a workshop for children and send them appropriately dressed. The teacher did everything she could to ensure that Jane had an apron on; if the child then chose to discard it half-way through, the teacher could hardly be expected to realize this when she was involved with 29 other children! The teacher knows that these practical play activities are important to the children's development and learning; how dare the parent try to tell her otherwise! And so on! In the meantime, the child who has no doubt enjoyed the gluing activity, perhaps made an excellent model and was feeling quite pleased with the result, finds herself the subject of dissension between her loved parent and her respected teacher.

The same kind of conflict for the child is apparent in the second scenario, perhaps even more seriously. This parent obviously does not understand what Whitbread (1987:227) calls the difference between 'sex identity and sex role stereotyping'. It was perhaps unfortunate that opportunity was not afforded the teacher to explain her carefully conceived rationale for the activity and possibly explore the parent's views on gender suitability. Had the teacher known this parent better, the situation could no doubt have been avoided, certainly to the advantage of the child, whose interest in knitting then had to be suspended indefinitely. (It would have been unwise of the teacher to pursue the activity in the classroom setting for fear of generating greater conflicts for the child.) This particular teacher had reasoned justification for the activity, but teachers are often in danger of defending play rather than justifying it and need to spend more time themselves in analysing just what play is providing for children both within the defined curriculum and in aspects of the 'hidden' curriculum. A Newsletter or Information Sheet to parents outlining some of the current topics and activities being explored in school through explanations, photographs and children's recorded activities, can generate interest, useful objects or materials and enquiries and, in this particular case, could have perhaps pre-empted an uncomfortable and disturbing confrontation all round. Care needs to be taken in the presentation of such documents, so that the tacit values it imparts are shared by all the school staff. The teacher in the third scene above gives implicit messages regarding work, play and associated learning, which may not be shared by others in the school. If such confused messages are presented to already confused parents, this can only exacerbate any unease and concerns they already have.

Shared perceptions

Even if the processes of early education are clearly explained to parents, we cannot expect them all to fully understand the intricate workings of the classroom, nor do they need to. But this does not mean that teachers must not explain why certain activities occur and what they provide for children. In relation to play, the author has always found that six main factors elicit realization from parents and other adults of the importance of play:

1. Children are clearly motivated by play. For parents, this is evidenced in the fact that even food, shopping trips, visits to friends' houses (all important to adults) will not tempt an involved child away from a play activity.
2. Play allows one to make mistakes without feeling guilty. Parents readily accept that when something goes wrong they can fall back on 'Well, I wasn't really doing that seriously, but now I'll do it for real!' This allows them and a child at play not to 'lose face' or feel too badly about themselves.
3. Playing with an object or a thought enables adults and children to recognize what they already know, what they need to know and how they can achieve what they want to. The example given in the introductory chapter of the exploration of a new washing machine is a good example to give parents to help recognition of this factor.
4. Adults are inclined to learn through a play mode under certain circumstances. Buying new items of clothing, equipment or whatever, parents quickly recognize, if it is pointed out to them, that they first handle and explore their proposed purchase, that they look for differences and similarities within the selection, that they are affected by touch, smell, sight, sound and taste, depending on what they are buying, and that certain 'background' factors (did the salesperson have particularly winning ways!) affect both decisions and their feelings and memories about the purchase later. The relationship between what they do in this situation and children's play experiences is usually indisputable.
5. Play, in different guises, helps adults to work through problems. Different problems have different solutions, but adults under stress can be found vigorously digging the garden, engaging in sport, doodling on a pad while mental processes are operating or indeed talking, reminiscing or just daydreaming in a world of their own. Parallels in children's fantasy and pretend play abound.
6. As well as learning, play occupies a recreational position for adults and children. Some recreational activities can be seen to be goal-directed, such as knitting, sewing, drawing, painting, modelling, mending the car, cooking, doing the garden, and so on. Several of these are also

Plate 13. Playing with an object or thought enables adults and children to recognize what they already know, what they need to know and how they can achieve what they want to.

undertaken for their intrinsic satisfaction, e.g. knitting, painting or drawing – and sports, television, reading, theatre and cinema would also be included in this list. Parents readily understand that learning occurs within all of these activities, whatever the intended original purpose.

Parents are particularly predisposed to understand play and its learning potential if invited to curriculum or topic sessions in school and allowed to experience for themselves some of the materials and resources children use. The timing of these sessions depends entirely on when a particular school feels its parents are most likely to be able to attend, but generally some parents will be available in the day and some only in the evenings, so it may be necessary to consider repeats. Parents seem to appreciate and understand the purpose of these sessions better if some activities are designed for them rather than expecting them to play like the children. The session needs also to contain some brief input explaining the school's view of play and time for parents to explore the issues. A few examples of activities used successfully with parents include:

1. *A pictorial or other language alphabet.* This helps parents to recognize the skills and processes required of a young reader. Playing games with the new words and associated pictures, letters and letter clusters encountered, as well as very short books in this 'new' alphabet enables parents to understand the value of such games and activities very quickly and makes a great deal of sense to them.

2. *100 square and number patterns.* Parents are asked first to decide and then to find out using a one-hundred board and plain and coloured tags, what pattern emerges by taking each third, fifth, ninth, etc., space on the board – surprisingly difficult for some.

3. *Cubic numbers.* Shown a single multi-link cube, parents are asked 'How many cubes are needed to make the next sized cube and the next one to that?' A majority will actually have to play with the cubes in order to really be positive of their answers.

4. *The fiveness of five* (could be any number but finger plays are particularly useful for five). Parents are presented with a large figure 5 and asked to explain what it means. Having explored a range of meanings, including the fact that it is only a symbol which represents something else, parents are then presented with 5 in a variety of other situations, such as on a house door (with three and seven on either side!), on a coin, on a weight, on the back of a sport's shirt, on a knitting pattern, as a word, and so on. Parents are asked to reflect on what challenges this may present to a child and what they and teachers do to try to resolve this – finger plays, laying the table for five, making different patterns of five and such like.

5. *When is a box not a box?* A variety of junk boxes are given to parents who first have to draw what the opened box might look like and then have to open out the box carefully to find out what the final net is really like.

6. *Making a triple-intersected Venn diagram.* A box of attribute blocks and the question 'Find something which fits in the middle intersection', creates great fun, interest and challenges.

7. *Snakes and ladders variations.* An adult version can easily be devised which asks such questions as 'Do you play with your children? – Go up the next ladder if yes, down the snake if no!' 'Do you know where to find a very hungry caterpillar – Go up the next ladder if yes, down the snake if no!' Many questions related to the activities of the school and the children can be devised and can be made to relate to the particular session's topic. Parents will recognize the necessity of both reading and discussion as vital to the procedures of the game.

8. *Checklists.* Participating adults can be given a list containing skills children will need to use, and can move around the available apparatus and resources placing its name at the side of the skill, e.g.:

The children will need to ...

Skill	Plaything
Spell words	Computer hangman game
Remember something	Kim's game
Count the objects	Laying the table
Learn to judge size	Dolls and dolls' clothes
Fit the pieces together	Lego, Clixi, Lasy A.
....	....

It cannot be stressed enough that, although the materials are those which the children will use, the activities require careful design so most parents are challenged in the way in which their children will be, rather than attempting to play like children. We cannot expect parents and other adults to emulate directly children's activities: they are at a different level and, after all, this is one of the factors being stressed – that we each operate from where we are now. At such sessions it is a good idea to show parents videos of their children in action with some of the materials they themselves have used. They are often quite staggered by what their children can do, especially if it is something with which they themselves had difficulty – as good an advertisement for directed play activities as anything! If teacher/child interaction is also a feature, the video can serve to deliver implicit but worthwhile messages regarding communicating with children about their play and the assessment of learning.

Different cultures, different expectations

Just as different religious beliefs prevail in our society, there is also a variation in the values associated with such aspects as play which tend to be culturally based. Within those cultures where children's labour is needed to support the family economy, play is unlikely to have any value, detracting as it does from the need to work for survival (see Whiting, 1963, for examples from different cultures). This is particularly likely to be the case for Asian families and, as cultural values remain even when people find themselves within a different host community, it is to be expected that Indian, Pakistani, Chinese and other such ethnic groups will attach only a non-work ethic to considerations of play. Teachers must ensure, through talking to parents, that they understand the relative values a particular ethnic group attaches to play, otherwise they are unlikely to be able to make adequate provision for the children. Communication with the maternal parent in particular, who is most likely due to family circumstances to play with the child, is complicated further by language differences. Yet communicate with these parents we must if we feel strongly that our play-based learning is appropriate and vital for all children.

I have found the kinds of play sessions with parents described above to work most satisfactorily with parents from different ethnic groups provided both parents are able to attend (mutual discussion later is vital); any handouts, games, instructions are conveyed in appropriate languages; and any talk uses a translator to ensure clarity of the message imparted and that questions receive an adequate response. It is vital to ensure, at least in the early days of explaining play (to all parents), that the links between play and the basic curriculum are made explicit. Hand skills – drawing, sewing, painting, tracing, and so on – are a vital prerequisite to writing in any language. Playing in the home corner, dressing different-sized dolls, measuring water and sand, all contribute to children's mathematical understanding, and direct relationships with numbers (counting and matching cups to hooks) are easily recognized.

It is of vital importance to all young children in a multicultural society such as ours that they have the opportunity to explore other cultures through artefacts, clothing, stories and festivals, and parents from different ethnic groups can be invaluable in giving advice and information on making multicultural provision in the home corner or shop. This is a natural way to engage these parents, ensuring a sense of value coupled with a purpose for communication. In helping the teacher to set up a particular shop or play 'home', for example, a parent will be encouraged to see that the play situation is carefully conceived to maximize learning and will be able to communicate this to other parents.

Other ways to involve parents in play

Just in the way that some parents help with children's reading in the classroom, willing parents can be given play tasks to undertake. If, however, the purpose is to enable a better understanding of the value of play, the parent must be given brief guidelines suggesting:

- the objectives for the play;
- the vocabulary which is to be promoted;
- other material which may be introduced and needs to be to hand; and
- how it might be expected that the children will respond.

For example, a parent asked to help children understand something of the concept of capacity in the sand tray, may initially be provided with the wet sand tray, a few different-sized containers and scoops. The objectives might be that the children will understand that the bigger container holds more and the smaller container less. The vocabulary needs anticipated might be sand, containers, full, empty, holds more, holds less, holds the same. Tall thin containers and flatter, thicker containers may be available for those children whose thinking needs extending, and one response of the children might be to try to make different-sized sandcastles. These variables could easily be transmitted on a card or sheet to the participating parent. A collection of such cards will soon accrue and prove themselves handy for any involved adults.

Toy Libraries are a very obvious way of ensuring parents come into contact with play materials, but even where these are not feasible the play resources bought for school can be displayed for parents and brief explanations of the purpose of the items can be given on bright cards, perhaps accompanied by photographs of children at play with that particular item. Toy Libraries are particularly beneficial to parents from different ethnic backgrounds and, if associated with a Parent and Toddler group, can often encourage these parents to both engage in play with their youngest children and socialize with other parents.*

Parents' 'make and play' sessions are useful ways of encouraging parents both to value play and actually play! The idea is that, under the advice of the head or available teacher, a group of parents gets together to make interesting and well-presented games for the children culled from a variety of sources (e.g. Baker, 1980; Williams and Somerwill, 1982). These can then be incorporated into a games library from which parents can select games to take home and play with the children, or parents could be encouraged to play with children in school. Either way the children benefit!

Inviting new parents in to the nursery or reception class to participate in the children's activities, is an excellent way of encouraging parents to see the value in play. It is particularly useful where crèche facilities (perhaps organized by another parent in a spare classroom or free area) allow parents to visit without their own children because they can usually be more objective about the children of others. Similarly, sessions where new parents attend in small groups and join in the class's activities a few weeks after their child has started in that class, are helpful in showing parents where play 'fits in' and that teachers do want to share their expertise. This works well where the head or a teacher without class responsibility can oversee the classroom activities while the normal class teacher talks to the parents about the children's activities.

Encouraging understanding and cooperation

It appears so far that the emphasis is on what teachers can do for parents and other interested adults and, in a sense, this has to be so. School is traditionally the teacher's territory and if parents are really to understand

---

* Very useful information is available on setting up Toy Libraries in multicultural schools from Ruth Gender, Family Education Unit, Rushymead Centre, Harrison Road, Leicester.

its processes as many wish to do, then they must in some way enter at least into its ethos. This is not to say that teachers should not equally value the home milieu. As Gilkes (1987:107) points out, staff with a genuine desire to work closely with parents for the good of the children, need to 'understand the families and be adaptable, flexible, non-judgemental and caring and understanding'. Teachers of young children are often the first people on a regular basis to intervene in the parent/child relationship and it is fair to say that some parents cannot cope with sharing a child for whom they have previously been totally responsible. If the child is not to be drawn in to 'sides', it is imperative that the teacher quickly builds a relationship with the parents, perhaps visiting them in their home and, equally, inviting them into the classroom social setting of which their child will be a member. There is now a good deal of accumulated evidence for home/school links being associated with the advancement of a child's education and attitudes to learning, particularly in relation to reading projects such as those instigated in Haringey and Belfield [see Bloom (1987) for an overview, and Hannon and Jackson (1987) and Schofield (1979) for direct analyses]. Information on the lasting effects on children's educational achievements of parental involvement are by now well-known through both the Headstart and Ypsilanti Perry Pre-School Projects (see Weikart, *et al.*, 1978; Zigler and Valentine, 1979). The extensive British study by Osborn and Milbank (1987) covers several features of children's enhanced learning through parental involvement and mentions mother involvement in pre-school provision as having a significant effect on children's later school success. Several researchers have pointed to the apparent superiority of parents in the education and development of their children (Grotberg, 1979) and particularly for children's language development (Tizard and Hughes, 1984; Wells, 1985b).

Arkinstall (1987:163) reminds us that 'the partnership between parents and teachers will never be an equal one because the parents and the teachers have different roles to play', but they can and must meet each other half-way by accepting such differences and each not trying to emulate but complement the other.

Concluding remarks

We are all inculculated in the views of our prevailing culture and these are inevitably historically based. From the onset of state education in 1870, the basic skills of literacy and numeracy have dominated adult thought in relation to school learning. These values still hold today (Farquhar *et al.*, 1985), not only for the indigenous society but for the different ethnic groups who have become part of that society. They persist because the products of education continue to hold paramountcy over its processes. Part of the reason for this is that up until relatively recently teachers, through accountability and examination systems have, in a sense, been required to emphasize *what* they do rather than *how* they achieve it. At secondary level, the continuous assessment associated with the relatively new examination system attaches less emphasis to the examination itself and therefore to the product, giving status to the processes involved in later achievement. In the early years, the emphasis now on teachers continuing and sustaining a child's education already begun at home and in the wider community, has meant a greater need for sharing the prerequisites of learning with parents and others. Play is just one such prerequisite if parents and other adults can be encouraged to attach to it appropriate values.

By encouraging parental (and other adult) involvement in as many ways as seems appropriate to particular school circumstances, we are doing more for the child than any amount of basic skills teaching, as Dowling (1988:98) suggests: 'Parents who do not have a stake in their children's early education place a heavy responsibility on the nursery or school to succeed alone.'

The question is not 'Can we do so?' but 'Is this right for the child?' Whatever the difficulties faced by all parties, the child needs the kind of concordance and cooperation that real partnership with parents requires, particularly in relation to the value attached to the child's play. It is particularly important that we take note of parent's views and ensure that these are always taken into consideration when decisions regarding curriculum, activities, play or whatever else are taken, but as Katz (1985:67) points out: 'There is a distinction between being sensitive to parents' expectations and capitulating to them.'

A rather amusing paradox exists in relation to adults' and children's views on play in school: as many teachers will know, when children are asked about what their parents and other adults do to earn a living, they just do not believe that teachers actually work! 'But you're with us all day!' is the usual response. Conversely, parents hardly ever believe that their children are 'working' in a play-based approach to learning. Somewhere here there is a serious message for all concerned.

Parental responsibility and involvement in schools is now a legislated reality: parental participation still has some way to go, as lavish attempts to encourage parents on to governing bodies indicates. Parent-governors of primary schools will need an understanding not only of the curriculum but the way the curriculum principles are put into practice, particularly through the process of play. This puts a heavy burden on teachers who, according to Woodhead (1981:250), need to ensure that they are the vital link in the chain as facilitators of learning through all interactions in and out of school.

10

Play in Childhood
and Adulthood

For richer or poorer?

No doubt however strong the arguments for children's and adults' play, there will still be sceptics who see no value in it at least as far as education is concerned. The usual argument is that sooner or later children have got to get used to the world of work, unpleasurable though it may be, and the sooner the better. This is ill-conceived and denies children the right to a balanced and relevant childhood in adopting a view of children as 'adults in waiting' (Dowling, 1987:10). It is also unrealistic in a generation which has seen a rapid decline in full employment and an expansion in leisure time, a generation which has also seen an increase in vandalism and violence apparently associated, at least in part, with people's lack of knowledge of how to use non-work time effectively and satisfyingly. Play is not as escape from life: it is an integral part of living (Schiller, 1954) and enables us all to understand ourselves and our lives better. 'Play schematizes life' according to Sutton-Smith and he believes that 'It has been a great mistake of Western theorizing to see play as simply an imitation of life' (Sutton-Smith, 1986:138–9).

The majority of people who do engage in adult play bouts – hobbies, sports, playing card and board games, games of chance, computer and video games, exploring new materials, places and situations, to name but a few play activities – need to consider how far their lives would be the poorer if such opportunities did not exist, for activity or escapism. If the answer is 'considerably so!', then why do we sometimes seek to deny play opportunities to our children and also not encourage greater play opportunities for adults? The kind of 'macho', competitive play engaged in by, for example, sports people, is revered by many and there is no denying the sense of achievement at success, the coming to terms with frustration when things do not quite happen as expected, or the physical well-being felt when relaxing after mental and physical stimulation. Why, however, do we attribute these feelings, experiences and satisfactions to adults, give them our approval and even admiration, but then seek to deny

Plate 14. The majority of people who do engage in adult play bouts need to consider how far their lives would be the poorer if such opportunities did not exist.

similar opportunities for success, physicality and the coming to terms with reality to our children? Although they are not simply mini-adults, children are people with directly comparable feelings, emotions, social and intellectual needs to adults, albeit with a greater immaturity and naïvety. Why, in this case, do we frequently expect children to do things we would hate to do ourselves and in which we can see no purpose? If we engage in some activity of importance to us, we would be more than a little enraged if someone constantly denied or put a stop to what we were doing! Figure 10.1 outlines a few of the basic needs of children. Adults should read down the list and, in the appropriate column, tick those aspects they themselves equally need. This may produce some surprises!

In school, basic skills and basic needs must work in tandem. This is where directed play is so vital. Certain basic needs can be met through free play and some basic skills will also be developed in this way, but many more require children to be set challenges and goals to enhance their self-image, self-confidence, sense of achievement and basic skill abilities. In Clark's (1988:277) study, she reports:

> Observational studies have shown that a free-play setting has potential for stimulating learning in young children ... it must be

Tick if your
own are similar

Have sleep and rest . . . .
Be warm and comfortable outside
  and inside! . . . .
Enjoy good food and drinks! . . . .
Have fresh air and exercise . . . .
Enjoy good health and healthy living . . . .
Enjoy a sense of physical and mental well-
  being and enjoy life . . . .
Opportunity to talk and develop language
  and communication . . . .
Engagement with books, pictures, poetry, the
  written word generally . . . .
Write, draw and generally make marks . . . .
Enjoy songs, music, sounds . . . .
Try out new words, phrases, vocabulary and
  new terminology . . . .
Imitate others/try out their ways . . . .
Occasions in which to be noisy . . . .
Opportunity to love and be loved . . . .
Opportunity to care for self and others . . . . . .
Occasions for being tender and loving . . . .
Interactions generally with other people of
  all ages and kinds . . . .
Opportunity to be aggressive . . . .
                    destructive . . . .
                    constructive . . . .
                    an observer . . . .
                    creative . . . .
                    adventurous . . . .
                    competitive . . . .
                    successful . . . .
                    physically energetic . . . .
                    physically relaxed . . . .
                    mentally challenged . . . .
                    mentally relaxed . . . .
                    alone . . . .
Withdraw from the immediate world . . . .
Use imagination . . . .
Daydream and have wishes fulfilled . . . .
Have friends and be sociable . . . .
Explore and investigate new experiences and
  opportunities . . . .
Handle different objects and touch things . . . . . .
Use sense of smell and taste . . . .
Enjoy visually appealing sights . . . .
Have curiosity satisfied . . . .
Have all senses stimulated . . . .
Appreciate humour and be humorous . . . .
Be possessive and acquisitive sometimes! . . . .

Be YOURSELF! . . . .

Fig. 10.1. Young children's fundamental needs.

carefully structured with the adults playing a crucial role in its organisation and by selective intervention with the children in their 'play'.

She goes on to say that most children need greater challenges in their play than currently exist. As with other learning, there are standards to be set in play, expectations of good quality play inevitably being met and the learning environment made the richer for it.

Playing with children

Strong evidence now exists, and has been already fairly extensively quoted, to suggest that children's play is enhanced and deepened by adult intervention. One such study by Tamburrini (1982:215) concluded that teachers who interact with children in their play and adopt an 'extending' style which synchronizes with the children's own intentions, is educationally profitable and, at the same time, values children's play in its own right. A clear message of support for what has been said throughout this book. Interaction does, however, require that adults enjoy and value playing with children. The implicit messages generated by those who do not are all too clear to a child and adults should examine why it is that they find play so tedious. There is some evidence to suggest that the 'work ethic' has a large part to play in this and that deep-down the adults concerned still do not feel that play has value.

Being equal partners in play, as in conversation, is vital to the generation of feelings of support from both or all parties. Even in directing play, the approach should be to offer 'I wonder what would happen ...?' type statements or provide tangible evidence of the adult's own play such as a pre-constructed model. (Half finished attempts or very simple, adaptable structures are superior if this method is used, because what is needed is not emulation but children who will bring their own interpretation, knowledge and imagination to bear.) Equal partners means equally valuing what each other does and children are more likely to respond to adults whom they respect and trust as fellow players. It will eventually revert back to what we, as teachers and other adults involved with young children, value. If we only value 'work' and written recording of it, then we will devote all our time and attention to this aspect of our own work. However, there is much research already reported herein which suggests that our emphasis is misguided and, occasionally, quite harmful to children's learning. For example, it is very easy to suffer boredom and a consequent dislike of learning, if one is expected to think in the abstract at a time when the ability to do so is limited. In Scandinavia, where children engage in nursery education and associated play activities up to the age of 7 years, there is virtually no adult illiteracy. Lally (1988:13) asks the questions:

Why then do we want to expose our children to teaching styles which failed many of us in the past? And why are we so reluctant to accept that we learn most from experiences which interest and motivate us and are fun?

Showing that play has, and can have, direction, progression and sound educational outcomes as well, should serve to convince all adults, including parents, that it is a worthwhile activity rightly associated with learning.

Many teachers appear to find the 'untidiness' of learning through play difficult to accept; not untidiness in the visual or practical sense, but in the lack of neat packages of 'learning', and the urge is to progress children very quickly to schemes of work where 'neatness' is in-built into the structure. We must resist this desire for ultimate 'order' if we are attempting to serve the needs of the children. Five-year-olds do not suddenly cease to need sand, water and social play: developmentally, they have only just begun to explore the potentialities of such media. What they need is more directed play through controlled resources to learn more from their position of current knowledge. Neither does the need for this type of activity cease at 8 years of age if teachers continue to give their attention to the learning potentialities within such media and are prepared to direct learning.

What is clear is that play must *never* be offered as a reward for 'work'. This devalues the role of play and gives absolute, definitive messages to children, parents and other adults about the school's view of education: that it can only take place through school work. This, as we have seen in Chapter 9, denies the educative role previously and continuously played by parents. Yet, equally, we must hold on to the fact that children's play in school is seminally different from the kind of play which children undertake when left to their own devices (Sutton-Smith and Kelly-Byrne, 1984) and should be so because of the accountability structure within which teachers must operate. After all, if we accept Kamii and DeVries's view, the function of the teacher is to '*provide materials, suggest activities and assess what is going on inside the child's head from moment to moment*' (Kamii and DeVries, 1977:406; original emphasis).

Finale

This has not basically been a book about *what* to do in regard to play or even *how* to do it for the most part: teachers know these things only too well and, as trained professionals, need to use their skills to provide the activities and the means to foster learning through play. Rather, the book has been about *why*: why should we encourage, promote, value and initiate play in our classrooms, why should we ourselves be part of it?

Hopefully, the book has explored some teachers' and other adults' many questions and concerns about the issue of play and readers will be prompted to turn to some of the excellent and informative texts on both the philosophy and processes of play mentioned herein. The move towards presenting early educators with principles rather than recipes for classroom practice (e.g. Bruce, 1987; Curtis, 1986; Dowling, 1988) is to be welcomed. Equally within this book, an attempt has been made to give some principles in relation to play and the other facets of early childhood education, while at the same time providing some support for putting these principles into practice.

Because of the lack of 'tidiness' in relation to play already explored above, it is not possible for a book of this nature to lay down neat classroom 'rules' in regard to play. It can merely explore the processes which may help play to function more effectively in more classrooms in terms of enhancing children's learning and development. Indeed, there are many issues which the book has not even attempted to mention but which are worthy of future study, e.g. if adults could be encouraged more to play with children and to understand their development and needs, would incidences of child abuse be reduced? What are the barriers to adult involvement in children's play: is it time, interest, motivation...? Play could certainly be an issue in reducing gender stereotyping in society not least through exploration of how greater interaction in play between the sexes from an early age could be further encouraged and what resources might, therefore, need to be provided.

Throughout, the term 'toys' has been deliberately avoided as far as possible. Toys are children's learning resources and they actively engage with such materials: it is almost disparaging to consider them as 'toys' given the connotation inherent in the word. It is difficult enough sometimes to overcome the terminology of 'play' and I am much in favour of 'working in the sand' or 'working with the bricks' to counteract the difficulties of children apparently 'playing' all day. In the long term, however, it reverts to the fact that play as such needs to be accepted for its value to children and to adults. As Millar (1968:256) says: 'Adults sometimes just "play", but children just "play" far more.'

The book has, however, attempted to give some other very clear messages in regard to play. Play in school is and should be very different from play in the home: parents have a right to expect this, and variety and interest can be maintained for children in both environments. Play covers all of a child's development in these two circumstances if it is properly understood and provided for in both. Play will inevitably take on a different register and appropriateness in the two circumstances, as indeed it will during other episodes of play such as in street or park with peers. In school, play can be exploratory, free or directed, the essential element being that, in whatever form, it should take the children forward from

Plate 15. Toys are children's learning resources and they actively engage with such materials.

where they are now in their learning through a process of trial and error, where error is treated as a vital learning process in itself. Teachers must develop in themselves the skills required, through observation of children in different activities, to decide what learning is taking place within play behaviours. They can also consider curriculum coverage, not in terms of looking for a play curriculum but through viewing play as a process and mode wherein children will exhibit certain behaviours. Children between the ages of 4 and 8 years play as naturally as they eat and sleep and learn significantly from that play, but they also learn in other ways which are playful and one essential role of the educators is to ensure that activities appear so. Finally, adults and children both play, and wherever possible it is beneficial to both sides if they play together, thus ensuring greater understanding of each other's feelings, attitudes, thoughts and differences.

Perhaps the ultimate difference between children's and adults' play is neatly summed up in one final thought: *Children play to encounter reality: adults play to avoid it!*

References

Almy, M. (1977). Piaget in action. *In* Smart, M. and Smart, R. (Eds), *Readings in Child Development and Relationships*. New York: Macmillan.

Arkinstall, M. (1987). Towards a partnership: The Taylor Report, School Government and Parental Involvement. *In* Lowe, R. (Ed.), *The Changing Primary School*. Lewes: Falmer Press.

Armstrong, M. (1980). *Closely Observed Children: The Diary of a Primary Classroom*. London and Richmond: Writers and Readers in association with Chameleon.

Arnberg, L. (1987). *Raising Children Bilingually: The Pre-school Years*. Bristol: Multilingual Matters.

Attenborough, D. (1988). *Wildlife on One*. 28 March. BBC Television.

Baker, C. (1980). *Reading Through Play*. London: Macdonald Educational.

Ballard, K.D. and Crooks, T.J. (1985). Individual preference for peer interaction: Some data on the self-report measure for pre-school children. *Exceptional Child*, **32**(2), 81–6.

Bate, M., Smith, M. and James, J. (1982). *Review of Tests and Assessments in Early Education (3–5 Years)*. Windsor: NFER/Nelson.

Bee, H. (1985). *The Developing Child*, 4th edn. New York: Harper and Row.

Bee, H. and Mitchell, S. (1988). The developing child: Stages of development in childhood. *In* Cohen, A. and Cohen, L. (Eds), *Early Education: The Pre-school Years. A Sourcebook for Teachers*. London: Paul Chapman.

Bekoff, M. and Byers. J.A. (1981). A critical analysis of the ontogeny and phylogeny of mammalian social and locomotor play: An ethological hornet's nest. *In* Immelman, K., Barlow, G.W., Petrinovich, L. and Main, M. (Eds), *Behavioural Development*. Cambridge: Cambridge University Press.

Bennett, N. (1976). *Teaching Styles and Pupil Progress*. London: Open Books.

Bennett, N., Desforges, C., Cockburn, A. and Wilkinson, B. (1984). *The Quality of Pupil Learning Experiences*. Hillsdale, N.J.: Lawrence Erlbaum Associates.

Berlyne, D.E. (1965). *Structure and Direction in Thinking*. New York: John Wiley.

Bettleheim, B. (1981). What happens when a child plays? *In* Strom, R. (Ed.), *Growing Through Play: Readings for Parents and Teachers*. Monterey, Calif.: Brooks/Cole.

Blatchford, P., Battle, S. and Mays, J. (1982). *The First Transition: Home to Pre-school*. Windsor: NFER/Nelson.

Bloom, W. (1987). *Partnership with Parents in Reading*. London: Hodder and Stoughton/UKRA.

Bradley, L. and Bryant, P. (1985). *Rhyme and Reason in Reading and Spelling*. Ann Arbor, Mich.: University of Michigan Press.

Branthwaite, A. and Rogers, D. (Eds) (1985). *Children Growing Up*. Milton Keynes: Open University Press.

Brennan, W.K. (1979). *Curricular Needs of Slow Learners*. London: Evans/ Methuen for School Council.

Brierley, J. (1987). *Give Me a Child Until He is Seven*. Lewes: Falmer Press.

Bright Ideas for Language Development (1984). Leamington Spa: Scholastic Publications/Ward Lock Educational.

Bronfenbrenner, U. (1979). Forward. *In* Chance, P., *Learning Through Play*. New York: Gardner Press.

Brown, A.L. and Campione, J.C. (1978). The effects of knowledge and experience on retrieval plans for studying from texts. *In* Gruneberg, M.M., Morris, P.E. and Sykes, R.N. (Eds), *Practical Aspects of Memory*. London and San Diego: Academic Press.

Bruce, T. (1987). *Early Childhood Education*. London: Hodder and Stoughton.

Bruner, J.S. (1971). The growth and structure of skill. *In* Connolly, K.J. (Ed.), *Motor Skills in Infancy*. London and San Diego: Academic Press.

Bruner, J.S. (1972). The nature and uses of immaturity. *American Psychol.* **27**, 687–708.

Bruner, J.S. (1973). *The Relevance of Education*. New York: W.W. Norton.

Bruner, J.S. (1977). Introduction. *In* Tizard, B. and Harvey, D. (Eds), *The Biology of Play*. London: Spastics International Medical Publications.

Bruner, J.S., Olver, R.R. and Greenfield, P.M. (1976). *Studies in Cognitive Growth*. New York: John Wiley.

Bruner, J.S., Jolly, A. and Sylva, K. (Eds) (1977). *Play: Its Role in Development and Evolution*. Harmondsworth: Penguin.

Burghardt, G.M. (1984). On the origins of play. *In* Smith, P.K. (Ed.), *Play in Animals and Humans*. Oxford: Basil Blackwell.

Burns, M. (1987). Reactions to problem solving. *In* Fisher, R. (Ed.), *Problem Solving in Primary Schools*. Oxford: Basil Blackwell.

Carey, S. (1974). Cognitive competence. *In* Connolly, K. and Bruner, J. (Eds), *The Growth of Competence*. London and San Diego: Academic Press.

Case, R. (1982). *Intellectual Development: A Systematic Reinterpretation*. London and San Diego: Academic Press.

Chazan, M. and Laing, A. (1982). *The Early Years*. Milton Keynes: Open University Press.

Chazan, M., Laing, A. and Harper, G. (1987). *Teaching Five to Eight Year Olds*. Oxford: Basil Blackwell.

Child, D. (1985). The growth of intelligence and creativity in young children. *In* Branthwaite, A. and Rogers, D. (Eds), *Children Growing Up*. Milton Keynes: Open University Press.

Clark, M.M. (Ed.) (1985). *Helping Communication in Early Education*. Educational Review Occasional Publication No.11, Faculty of Education, University of Birmingham.

Clark, M.M. (1988). *Children Under Five: Educational Research and Evidence*. London: Gordon and Breach.

Claxton, G. (1984). *Live and Learn: An Introduction to the Psychology of Growth and Change in Everyday Life*. London: Harper Row.

Cleveland Enquiry (1988). *Report of the Enquiry into Child Abuse in Cleveland 1987*. Chair–Rt Hon Lord Justice Butler-Sloss Cmnd 412. London: HMSO.

Clifford, A. (1983). Pupils, parents and teachers: The dynamics of relationships. *Early Child Development and Care*, **11**(3/4), 275–83.

Coates, E. (1985). An examination of the nature of young children's discussions. *In* Clark, M.M. (Ed.), *Helping Communication in Early Education*. Educational Review Occasional Publication No.11, Faculty of Education, University of Birmingham.

Cohen, A. and Cohen, L. (Eds) (1988). *Early Education: The Pre-school Years. A Sourcebook for Teachers*. London: Paul Chapman.

Cohen, D. (1987). *The Development of Play*. London: Croom Helm.

Cohen, N. (1988). Guilty Secrets. Report on the work of Madge Bray. *Times Educational Supplement*, 5 February, p. 25.

Combs, A.W. (1982). *A Personal Approach to Teaching: Beliefs that Make a Difference*. Boston: Allyn and Bacon.

Connolly, K. and Bruner, J.S. (Eds) (1974). *The Growth of Competence*. London and San Diego: Academic Press.

Crayhay, M. (1980). *Characteristiques Socio-Culturelles de la Population Scolaire et Curriculum Realise dans Quatres Classes Maternelles*. Document de Travail. Laboratoire de Pedagogie Experimentale. University de Liege, Belgium.

Croll, P. (1984). *Systematic Classroom Observation*. Lewes: Falmer Press.

Cummins, J. (1982). Mother-tongue maintenance for minority language children: Some common misconceptions. Paper prepared for a Conference on Bilingualism and Education. Aberystwyth, September.

Currie, M. and Foster, L. (1975). *Classes and Counts*. Teaching 5 to 13 series. London: Macdonald.

Curtis, A. (1986). *A Curriculum for the Pre-School Child: Learning to Learn*. Windsor: NFER/Nelson.

Curtis, A. and Wignall, M. (1981). *Early Learning: Assessment and Development*. London: Macmillan.

Dansky, J.L. (1980). Make-believe: A mediator of the relationship between play and associative fluency. *Child Development*, **51**, 576–9.

Danksy, J.L. and Silverman, I.W. (1977). Effects of play on associative fluency in pre-school children. *In* Bruner, J.S., Jolly, A. and Sylva, K. (Eds), *Play: Its Role in Development and Evolution*. Harmondsworth: Penguin.

Davis, R. (1985). *A longitudinal study of developmental changes in children's problem solving strategies between 5 and 9 years*. Ph.D thesis, University of London Institute of Education.

Davis, R., Golby, M., Kernig, W. and Tamburrini, J. (1986). *The Infant School: Past, Present and Future*. Bedford Way Papers 27. London: Institute of Education.

Dawson, R. (1985). *Teachers' Guide to TIPs*. London: Macmillan.

Dean, J. (1983). *Organising Learning in the Primary School*. London: Croom Helm.

De Bono, E. (1972). *Children Solve Problems*. Harmondsworth: Penguin.

Department of Education and Science (1967). *The Plowden Report: Children and*

Their Primary Schools. Central Advisory Council for Education (England). London: HMSO.

Department of Education and Science (1978). *The Warnock Report: Special Education Needs.* London: HMSO.

Department of Education and Science (1981). *Curriculum from 5 to 16.* London: HMSO.

Department of Education and Science (1982a). *First School Survey: Education 5 to 9. An Illustrative Survey of 80 First Schools in England.* London: HMSO.

Department of Education and Science (1982b). *The Cockroft Report: Mathematics Counts.* London: HMSO.

Department of Education and Science (1985a). *Better Schools: A Survey.* London: HMSO.

Department of Education and Science (1985b). *The Swann Report: Education for All.* London: HMSO.

Department of Education and Science (1987a). *Primary Schools: Some Aspects of Good Practice.* London: HMSO.

Department of Education and Science (1987b). *The National Curriculum 5 to 16: A Consultation Document.* The Welsh Office. London: HMSO.

Department of Education and Science (1988a). *The Kingman Report: Report of the Committee of Inquiry into the Teaching of English Language.* London: HMSO.

Department of Education and Science (1988b). *The National Curriculum: Mathematics for Ages 5 to 16.* The Welsh Office. London: HMSO.

Department of Education and Science (1988c). *The National Curriculum: Science for Ages 5 to 16.* The Welsh Office. London: HMSO.

Desforges, C. and Cockburn, A. (1988). *Understanding the Mathematics Teacher: A Study of Practice in First Schools.* Lewes: Falmer Press.

Dombey, H. (1983). Learning the language of books. *In* Meek, M. (Ed.), *Opening Moves: Achievement in Writing at 16 +.* London: Schools Council.

Donaldson, M. (1978). *Children's Minds.* Glasgow: Fontana.

Dowling, M. (1987). Understanding under-fives. *Perspective: The Journal for Advisers and Inspectors*, October, pp. 8–10.

Dowling, M. (1988). *Education 3 to 5: A Teachers' Handbook.* London: Paul Chapman.

Doyle, K.O., Jr (1983). *Evaluating Teaching.* Lexington, Mass.: Lexington Books.

Duffin, J. (1987). The canoe problem. *In* Fisher, R. (Ed.), *Problem Solving in Primary Schools.* Oxford: Basil Blackwell.

Duncan, A. and Dunn, W. (1988). *What Primary Teachers Should Know About Assessment.* London: Hodder and Stoughton.

Dunn, J. and Wooding, C. (1977). Play in the home and its implications for learning. *In* Tizard, B. and Harvey, D. (Eds), *The Biology of Play.* London: Spastics International Medical Publications.

Edwards, D. and Mercer, N. (1987). *Common Knowledge: The Development of Understanding in the Classroom.* London: Methuen.

Edwards, V. (1983). *Language in Multicultural Classrooms.* London: Batsford.

El'Kounin, D. (1982). Symbolics and its functions in the play of children. *In* Herron, R.E. and Sutton-Smith, B. (Eds), *Child's Play.* New York: John Wiley.

Equal Opportunities Commission (n.d.). *Equal Start: Guidelines for Working with the Under-fives.* Manchester: EOC.

Erikson, E.H. (1950). *Childhood and Society.* New York: W.W. Norton.

Evertson, C.M. and Brophy, J.E. (1974). *The Texas Teacher Effectiveness Project.* An ERIC Report. Washington: National Institute of Education.

Farquhar, C., Blatchford, P., Burke, J., Plewis, I. and Tizard, B. (1985). Parents and teachers: A comparison of the views of parents and reception teachers. *Education 3–13*, **13**(2), 17–22.

Fein, G.G. (1981). Pretend play in childhood: An integrative view. *Child Development*, **52**(4), 1095–118.

Feitelson, D. (1977). Cross-cultural studies of representational play. *In* Tizard, B. and Harvey, D. (Eds), *The Biology of Play.* London: Spastics International Medical Publications.

Fisher, R. (Ed.) (1987). *Problem Solving in Primary Schools.* Oxford: Basil Blackwell.

Fontana, D. (Ed.) (1984). *The Education of the Young Child,* 2nd edn. London: Open Books.

Freyberg, J. (1981). Unpublished study. Quoted in Pulaski, M.A.S., The rich rewards of make believe. *In* Strom, R. (Ed.), *Growing Through Play: Readings for Parents and Teachers.* Monterey, Calif.: Brooks/Cole.

Froebel, F. (1826). *The Education of Man.* New York: Appleton.

Gagne, E.M. (1970). *The Conditions of Learning,* 2nd Edn. New York: Holt, Rinehart and Winston.

Galton, M., Simon, B. and Croll, P. (1980). *Inside the Primary Classroom.* London: Routledge and Kegan Paul.

Gardner, J.K. and Gardner, H. (1975). *Studies of Play: An Original Anthology.* NJ.: Ayer.

Garvey, C. (1977). *Play.* London: Fontana.

Gessell, A., Ilg, F.L. and Ames, L.B. (1973). *The Child from Five to Ten.* London: Hamish Hamilton.

Gilkes, J. (1987). *Developing Nursery Education.* Milton Keynes: Open University Press.

Goodnow, J. (1977). *Children's Drawings.* Glasgow: Collins/Fontana.

Groos, K. (1898). *The Play of Animals.* New York: Appleton.

Grotberg, E. (1979). The parental role in education and child development. *In* Doxiades, S. (Ed.), *The Child in the World Tomorrow.* Oxford: Pergamon.

Guilford, J.P. (1957). Creative abilities in the arts. *Psychological Review*, **64**, 110–18.

Halford, G.S. (1980). Towards a redefinition of cognitive developmental stages. *In* Kirby, J.R. and Biggs, J.B. (Eds), *Cognition, Development and Instruction.* London and San Diego: Academic Press.

Hall, N. (1987). *The Emergence of Literacy.* London: Hodder and Stoughton/ UKRA.

Halliday, J.K. (1975). *Learning How to Mean.* London: Edward Arnold.

Hannon, P. and Jackson, A. (1987). *The Belfield Reading Project: Final Report.* Belfield County Council/National Children's Bureau.

Hans, J.S. (1981). *The Play of the World.* Cambridge, Mass.: University of Massachusetts Press.

Hargreaves, D.H. (1975). *Interpersonal Relations and Education* (Student edition). London: Routledge and Kegan Paul.

Herron, R.E. and Sutton-Smith, B. (Eds) (1982). *Child's Play*. New York: John Wiley.

Holdaway, D. (1979). *The Foundations of Literacy*. Sydney: Ashton Scholastic.

Holt, J. (1972). *How Children Learn*. Harmondsworth: Penguin.

Holt, J. (1975). *Escape from Childhood*. Harmondsworth: Penguin.

Houlton, D. (1985). *All Our Languages: A Handbook for the Multilingual Classroom*. London: Edward Arnold.

Houlton, D. and Willey, R. (1985). *Supporting Children's Bilingualism*. Schools Council/SCDC Publications Prog. 4.

Hughes, M. (1986). *Children and Number*. Oxford: Basil Blackwell.

Hutchcroft, D. (1981). *Making Language Work*. Maidenhead: McGraw-Hill.

Hutt, C. (1966). *Exploration and Play in Children*. Symposia of the Zoological Society of London, 18. London and San Diego: Academic Press.

Hutt, C. (1979). Play in the under 5's: Form, development and function. *In* Howells, J.G. (Ed.), *Modern Perspectives in the Psychiatry of Infancy*. New York: Brunner/Marcel.

Hutt, C. (1982). Exploration and play in children. *In* Herron, R.E. and Sutton-Smith, B. (Eds), *Child's Play*. New York: John Wiley.

Hyland, D. (1984). *The Question of Play*. Lanham: University Press of America.

Ingram, D. (1988). Pupil experiences. *In* Lang, P. (Ed.), *Thinking About ... Personal and Social Education in the Primary School*. Oxford: Basil Blackwell.

Irwin, E. and Frank, H. (1981). Facilitating the play process with LD children. *In* Strom, R. (Ed.), *Growing Through Play: Readings for Parents and Teachers*. Monterey, Calif.: Brooks/Cole.

Isaacs, S. (1930). *Intellectual Growth in Young Children*. London: Routledge and Kegan Paul.

Jeanrenaud, C. and Bishop, D. (1980). Roadblocks to creativity through play. *In* Wilkinson, P. (Ed.), *In Celebration of Play: An Integrated Approach to Play and Child Development*. London: Croom Helm.

Johnson, J.E. (1976). Relations of divergent thinking and intelligence test scores with social and non-social make-believe play of pre-school children. *Child Development*, **47**, 1200–3.

Jowett, S. and Sylva, K. (1986). Does kind of pre-school matter. *Educational Research*, **28**(1), 21–31.

Kalverboer, A.F. (1977). Measurement of play: Clinical applications. *In* Tizard, B. and Harvey, D. (Eds), *The Biology of Play*. London: Spastics International Medical Publications.

Kamii, C. and DeVries, R. (1977). Piaget for early education. *In* Day, M.C. and Parker, R.K. (Eds), *The Pre-school in Action: Explaining Early Childhood Programs*. Boston: Allyn and Bacon.

Katz, L.G. (1985). Fostering communicative competence in young children. *In* Clark, M.M. (Ed.), *Helping Communication in Early Education*. Educational Review Occasional Publication No.11, Faculty of Education, University of Birmingham.

Kerry, T. and Tollitt, J. (1987). *Teaching Infants*. Oxford: Basil Blackwell.

King, R. (1978). *All Things Bright and Beautiful?* London: John Wiley.

Kirklees Metropolitan Council (1985). *Guidelines for the Curriculum in the Early Years: A Discussion Document.* Self published by Kirklees L.E.A.

Lally, M. (1988). 'Work is child's play'. *Times Educational Supplement.* 19 August, p.13.

Lancy, D.F. (1981). Play in species adaptation. *Annual Review of Anthropology*, **9**, 471–95.

Lee, C. (1977). *The Growth and Development of Children.* London: Longman.

Levy, A.K. (1984). The language of play: The role of play in language development. *Early Child Development and Care*, **17**(1), 49–61.

Lewis, M. (1982). Play as Whimsy. *Behavioural and Brain Sciences*, **5**, 166.

Lieberman, J.N. (1977). *Playfulness: Its Relationship to Imagination and Creativity.* London and San Diego: Academic Press.

Loizos, C. (1969). Play behaviour in higher primates: A review. *In* Morris, D. (Ed.), *Primate Ethology.* Chicago: Aldine.

Lowe, R. (Ed.) (1987). *The Changing Primary School.* Lewes: Falmer Press.

MacDonald, H.M. (1985). Sex differences in the development of cognitive ability. *In* Branthwaite, A. and Rogers, D. (Eds), *Children Growing Up.* Milton Keynes: Open University Press.

Maher, P. (Ed.) (1987). *Child Abuse: The Educational Perspective.* Oxford: Basil Blackwell.

Manning, K. and Sharp, A. (1977). *Structuring Play in the Early Years at School.* London: Ward Lock Educational/Schools Council.

Manning, M. and Herrmann, J. (1988). The relationships of problem children in nursery schools. *In* Cohen, A. and Cohen, L. (Eds), *Early Education: The Pre-school Years. A Sourcebook for Teachers.* London: Paul Chapman.

Marzollo, J. and Lloyd, J. (1972). *Learning Through Play.* London: George Allen and Unwin.

Meek, M. (1985). Play and paradoxes: Some considerations of imagination and language. *In* Wells, G. and Nicholls, J. (Eds), *Language and Learning: An Interactional Perspective.* Lewes: Falmer Press.

Millar, S. (1968). *The Psychology of Play.* Harmondsworth: Penguin.

Millman, J. (Ed.) (1981). *Handbook of Teacher Evaluation.* Beverley Hills, Calif.: Sage Publications.

Mohan, M. and Hull, R.E. (1972). *Teaching Effectiveness: Its Meaning, Assessment and Improvement.* Englewood Cliffs: Educational Technical.

Morris, D. (Ed.) (1969). *Primate Ethology.* Chicago: Aldine.

Moyles, J.R. (1986). The whole picture. *Child Education*, **62**(3), 10–11.

Moyles, J.R. (1988). *Self-evaluation: A Primary Teacher's Guide.* Windsor: NFER/Nelson.

Musselwhite, C.R. (1986). *Adaptive Play for Special Needs Children.* San Diego: College Hill Press.

Mussen, P.H., Conger, J.J. and Kagan, J. (1965). *Child Development and Personality.* New York: Harper and Row.

Nash, R. (1984). *Classrooms Observed.* London: Routledge and Kegan Paul.

National Writing Project (1988). *About Writing: The SCDC National Writing Project.* London: SCDC.

Needles, D.J. (1980). Dramatic play in early childhood. *In* Wilkinson, P. (Ed.),

In Celebration of Play: An Integrated Approach to Play and Child Development. London: Croom Helm.

Newson, E., Head, J. and Mogford, K. (1973). Play in the remediation of handicap. Unpublished Report, University of Nottingham.

Nisbet, J.D. and Shucksmith, J. (1986). *Learning Strategies.* London: Routledge and Kegan Paul.

Nord, J.R. (1980). Developing listening fluency before speaking: An alternative paradigm. *System*, **8**, 1–22.

Norman, D.A. (1978). Notes towards a complex theory of learning. *In* Lesgold, A.M. (Ed.), *Cognitive Psychology and Instructions.* New York: Plenum.

Opie, I. and Opie, P. (1959). *The Lore and Language of Schoolchildren.* Oxford: Clarendon Press.

Opie, I. and Opie, P. (1969). *Children's Games in Street and Playground.* Oxford, Clarendon Press.

Osborn, A.F. and Milbank, J.F. (1987). *The Effects of Early Education.* Oxford, Clarendon Press.

Peacocke, R.W. (1987). Education 4–9: Early childhood does not end at 5. *News From BAECE*, **17**, 4–5.

Pellegrini, A.D. (1985). The relations between symbolic play and literate behaviour: A review and critique of the empirical literature. *Review of Educational Research*, **55**(1), 107–21.

Pepler, D.J. (1982). Play and divergent thinking. *In* Pepler, D.J. and Rubin, K.H. (Eds), *The Play of Children: Current Theory and Research.* Basel: S. Karger.

Pepler, D.J. and Rubin, K.H. (Eds) (1982). *The Play of Children: Current Theory and Research.* Basel: S. Karger.

Piaget, J. (1926). *The Language and Thought of the Child.* London: Routledge and Kegan Paul.

Piaget, J. (1950). *The Psychology of Intelligence.* London: Routledge and Kegan Paul.

Piaget, J. (1951). *Play, Dreams and Imitation in Childhood.* London: Heinemann.

Piaget, J. (1966). Foreward. *In* Almy, M. (Ed.), *Young Children's Thinking.* New York: Teachers College Press.

Piers, M.W. and Landau, G.M. (1980). *The Gift of Play and Why Children Cannot Thrive Without it.* New York: Walker and Co.

Pluckrose, H. (1984). Learning and teaching art and craft skills. *In* Fontana, D. (Ed.), *The Education of the Young Child*, 2nd edn. London: Open Books.

Prosser, G. (1985). Play – a child's eye view. *In* Branthwaite, A. and Rogers, D. (Eds), *Children Growing Up.* Milton Keynes: Open University Press.

Pulaski, M.A.S. (1981). The rich rewards of make-believe. *In* Strom, R. (Ed.), *Growing Through Play: Readings for Parents and Teachers.* Monterey, Calif.: Brooks/Cole.

Richards, C. (1987). The Curriculum from 5–16: Background, content and some implications for primary education. *In* Southworth, G. (Ed.), *Readings in Primary School Management.* Lewes: Falmer Press.

Riess, A. (1981). Unpublished study. Quoted in Pulaski, M.A.S., The rich rewards of make-believe. *In* Strom, R. (Ed.), *Growing Through Play: Readings for Parents and Teachers.* Monterey, Calif.: Brooks/Cole.

Rosen, C. and Rosen, H. (1973). *The Language of Primary School Children*. Harmondsworth: Penguin.

Rubin, K.H. and Howe, N. (1985). Toys and play behaviours: An overview. *Topics in Early Childhood Special Education*, 5(3), 1-10.

Rutter, M. (1982). *Helping Troubled Children*. Harmondsworth: Penguin.

Saltzberger-Wittenberg, I., Gianna, H. and Osborne, E. (1983). *The Emotional Experience of Learning and Teaching*. New York: Routledge and Kegan Paul.

Saunders, G. (1982). *Bilingual Children: Guidance for the Family*. Multi-lingual Matters, 3. Clevedon, Avon.

Sava, S.G. (1975). *Learning Through Discovery for Young Children*. New York: McGraw Hill.

Schiller, F. (1945). *The Aesthetic Letters, Essays and the Philosophical Letters*. Boston: Little Brown.

Schiller, F. (1954). *On the Aesthetic Education of Man* (Trans. R. Snell). New Haven: York University Press.

Schofield, W. (1979). *Haringey Reading Project*. Final Report to the DES (unpublished).

Schools Council (1983). *Primary Practice: A Sequel to the Practical Curriculum*. Schools Council Working Paper No.75. London: Methuen.

Schwartzman, H.B. (1982). Play as a mode. *Behavioural and Brain Sciences*, 5, 168-9.

Shipman, M. (1983). *Assessment in Primary and Middle Schools*. London: Croom Helm.

Shuard, H. (1984). Mathematics in English primary schools. *The Elementary School Journal*, 84(5), 583-94.

Simon, T. (1985). Play and Learning with Computers. *Early Child Development and Care*, 19(1/2), 69-78.

Singer, D. and Singer, J. (1977). Family television viewing habits and the spontaneous play of pre-school children. *In* Smart, M. and Smart, R. (Eds), *Readings in Child Development and Relationships*, 2nd Edn. New York: Macmillan.

Singer, D. and Singer, J. (1981). Raising boys who know how to love. *In* Strom, R. (Ed.), *Growing Through Play: Readings for Parents and Teachers*. Monterey, Calif.: Brooks/Cole.

Sloboda, J. (1985). Infant perception. *In* Branthwaite, A. and Rogers, D. (Eds), *Children Growing Up*. Milton Keynes: Open University Press.

Smith, P.K. (1977). Social and fantasy play in young children. *In* Tizard, B. and Harvey, D. (Eds), *The Biology of Play*. London: Spastics International Medical Publications.

Smith, P.K. (1982). Does play matter? Functional and evolutionary aspects of animal and human play. *Behavioural and Brain Sciences*, 5(1), 139-84.

Smith, P.K. (Ed.) (1984). *Play in Animals and Humans*. Oxford: Basil Blackwell.

Smith, P.K. (1988). The relevance of fantasy play for development in young children. *In* Cohen, A. and Cohen, L. (Eds), *Early Education: The Pre-school Years*. London: P.C.P.

Smith, P.K. and Connolly, K. (1977). Social and aggressive behaviour in pre-school children as a function of crowding. *Social Sciences Information*, 16, 601-20.

Smith, P.K. and Connolly, K. (1980). *The Ecology of Pre-school Education.* Cambridge: Cambridge University Press.

Smith, P.K. and Green, M. (1975). Aggressive behaviour in English nurseries and play groups: Sex differences and response of adults. *Child Development,* **46**(1), 211–14.

Smith, P.K. and Simon, T. (1984). Object play, problem-solving and creativity in children. *In* Smith, P.K. (Ed.), *Play in Animals and Humans.* Oxford: Basil Blackwell.

Southworth, G. (Ed.) (1987). *Readings in Primary School Management.* Lewes: Falmer Press.

Stallibrass, A. (1974). *The Self-respecting Child.* London: Thames and Hudson.

Stern, C. (1987). The recognition of child abuse. *In* Maher, P. (Ed.), *Child Abuse: The Educational Perspective.* Oxford: Basil Blackwell.

Stevens, P. Jr (1977). Laying the groundwork for an anthropology of play. *In* Phillips-Stevens, Jr (Ed.), *Studies in the Anthropology of Play: Papers in Memory of B. Allan Tindale.* New York: Leisure Press.

Stone, G.P. (1982). The play of little children. *In* Herron, R.E. and Sutton-Smith, B. (Eds), *Child's Play.* New York: John Wiley.

Strom, R. (Ed.) (1981a). *Growing Through Play: Readings for Parents and Teachers.* Monterey, Calif.: Brooks/Cole.

Strom, R. (1981b). The merits of solitary play. *In* Strom, R. (Ed.), *Growing Through Play: Readings for Parents and Teachers.* Monterey: Calif.: Brooks/Cole.

Sutton-Smith, B. (1986). *Toys as Culture.* New York: Gardner Press.

Sutton-Smith, B. and Kelly-Byrne, D. (1984). The idealization of play. *In* Smith, P.K. (Ed.), *Play in Animals and Humans.* Oxford: Basil Blackwell.

Sylva, K. (1977). Play and Learning. *In* Tizard, B. and Harvey, D. (Eds.), *The Biology of Play.* London: Spastics International Medical Publications.

Sylva, K., Bruner, J.S. and Genova, P. (1977). The role of play in the problem-solving of children 3–5 years old. *In* Bruner, J.S., Jolly, A. and Sylva, K. (Eds), *Play: Its Role in Development and Evolution.* Harmondsworth: Penguin.

Sylva, K., Roy, C. and Painter, M. (1980). *Child Watching at Playgroup and Nursery School.* London: Grant McIntyre.

Tamburrini, J. (1982). Play and the role of the teacher. *Early Child Development and Care,* **8**(3/4), 209–17.

Tinbergen, N. (1976). *The Importance of Being Playful.* London: BAECE Publications 1.

Tizard, B. (1977). Play: The child's way of learning. *In* Tizard, B. and Harvey, D. (Eds), *The Biology of Play.* London: Spastics International Medical Publications.

Tizard, B. and Harvey, D. (Eds) (1977). *The Biology of Play.* London: Spastics International Medical Publications.

Tizard, B. and Hughes, M. (1984). *Young Children Learning: Talking and Thinking at Home and at School.* London: Fontana.

Tizard, B., Blatchford, P., Burke, J., Farquhar, C. and Plewis, I. (1988). *Young Children at School in the Inner City.* London: Lawrence Erlbaum Associates.

Tough, J. (1977a). *The Development of Meaning: A Study of Children's Use of Language.* London: Allen and Unwin.

Tough, J. (1977b). *Talking and Learning: A Guide to Fostering Communication Skills in Nursery and Infant School.* London: Ward Lock Education for Schools Council.

Turnure, J., Buium, N. and Thurlow, M. (1976). The effectiveness of interrogations for promoting verbal elaboration productivity in young children. *Child Development,* **11,** 780–7.

Vandenberg, B. (1986). Mere child's play. *In* Blanchard, K. (Ed.), *The Many Faces of Play.* The Association of the Anthropological Study of Play, Vol. 9. Champaign, Illinois: Human Kinetics.

Vygotsky, L.S. (1932). *Thought and Language.* Cambridge, Mass.: MIT Press.

Vygotsky, L.S. (1933). Play and its role in the mental development of the child. *In* Bruner, J.S., Jolly, A. and Sylva, K. (1977). *Play: Its Role in Development and Evolution.* Harmondsworth: Penguin.

Vygotsky, L.S. (1977). *Thinking and Speech* (Trans. A. Sutton). Centre for Child Study, University of Birmingham.

Vygotsky, L.S (1978). Mind in society: the development of higher psychological processes. *In* Cole, M., John-Steiner, V., Scribner, S. and Souberman, G. (Eds), *Mind in Society.* Cambridge, Mass.: Howard University Press.

Wagner, D.A. and Stevenson, H.W. (1982). *Cultural Perspectives on Child Development.* San Francisco: W.H. Freeman.

Wall, W.D. (1961). Meeting the deprivation imposed by handicap. *Special Education,* **50**(4), 24.

Webb, L. (1967). *Children with Special Needs in the Infants' School.* London: Collins/Fontana.

Weikart, D.P., Epstein, A.S., Schweinhart, L. and Bond, J.T. (1978). *The Ypsilanti Pre-school Curriculum Demonstration Project: Pre-school Years and Longitudinal Results.* Ypsilanti, Mich.: High/Scope Educational Research Foundation.

Weir, R.H. (1962). *Language in the Crib.* The Hague: Mouton.

Weisler, A. and McCall, R. (1976). Exploration and Play. *American Psychologist,* **31,** 492–508.

Wells, G. (1985a). *Language Development in the Pre-school Years.* Cambridge: Cambridge University Press.

Wells, G. (1985b). Language and learning. *In* Wells, G. and Nicholls, J. (Eds), *Language and Learning: An Interactional Perspective.* Lewes: Falmer Press.

Wells, G. (1986). *The Meaning-makers: Children Learning Language and Using Language to Learn.* New Hampshire: Heinemann Educational.

Wells, G. (1988). Language and learning: an interactional perspective. *In* Cohen, A. and Cohen, L. (Eds), *Early Years Education: The Pre-school Years.* London: Paul Chapman.

Wells, G. and Nicholls, J. (Eds) (1985). *Language and Learning: An Interactional Perspective.* Lewes: Falmer Press.

Wetton, P. (1983). Some observations of interest in locomotor and gross motor activity in nursery schools. *P.E. Review,* **6**(2), 124–9.

Wetton, P. (1988). *Physical Education in the Nursery and Infant School.* London: Croom Helm.

Whitbread, N. (1987). Gender in primary schooling. *In* Lowe, R. (Ed.), *The Changing Primary School.* Lewes: Falmer Press.

Whiting, B.B. (Ed.) (1963). *Six Cultures: Studies of Child Rearing.* New York: John Wiley.

Wiles, S. (1985). Language and learning in multi-ethnic classrooms: Strategies for supporting bilingual studies. *In* Wells, G. and Nicholls, J. (Eds), *Language and Learning: An Interactional Perspective.* Lewes: Falmer Press.

Wilkinson, P. (Ed.) (1980). *In Celebration of Play: An Integrated Approach to Play and Child Development.* London: Croom Helm.

Williams, M. and Somerwill, H. (1982). *40 Maths Games to Make and Play: The Early Years.* London: Macmillan Education.

Winkley, D. (1987). Passion and purposes: Curriculum design and the creation of meaning. *In* Lowe, R. (Ed.), *The Changing Primary School.* Lewes: Falmer Press.

Wood, D., McMahon, L. and Cranstoun, Y. (1980). *Working with Under Fives.* London: Grant McIntyre.

Wood, H. and Wood, D. (1983). Questioning the pre-school child. *Educational Review*, **35**(2), 149–62.

Woodhead, M. (1981). Cooperation in early education: What does it mean? Why does it matter? *Early Child Development and Care*, **7**(2/3), 235–52.

Woodhead, M. (1988). Let children be our guide. *Times Educational Supplement*, 12 August, p. 13.

Wragg, E.C. (1987). *Teacher Appraisal: A Practical Guide.* London: Macmillan.

Yardley, A. (1984). Understanding and encouraging children's play. *In* Fontana, D. (Ed.), *The Education of the Young Child*, 2nd edn. London: Open Books.

Zigler, E. and Valentine, J. (Eds) (1979). *Project Headstart: A Legacy of The War on Poverty.* New York: Free Press.

Index